I have been waiting for this book for YEARS. Laura is brilliant and brave and creative and wise. We've been friends since we were teenagers with ponytails and crushes, and these days, she's still the first one I'll text for a book recommendation. This book will be the starting point for so many meaningful conversations, because Laura knows connection comes from sharing our stories. She's been sharing her stories with me for more than twenty years, and I'm thrilled that so many people will be able to join that conversation now—it's one that has instructed me, challenged me, and healed me a thousand times over the years. Buy a copy of this book for every person in your life that you want to know in a deeper, more meaningful way.

Shauna Niequist, *New York Times*
bestselling author of *Present Over Perfect*

To the person who is afraid of being seen but desperately wants to be known, this book is a love letter to vulnerability, sparkling on every page. Laura goes first, masterfully telling her own stories, enthusiastically and lovingly pulling us by the hand to do the same, and you'll willingly follow her. The path is clear, the questions are illuminating, and deeper connection is inevitable. It's seriously *such* a great book.

Kendra Adachi, *New York Times*
bestselling author of *The Lazy Genius Way*
and host of *The Lazy Genius Podcast*

In this insightful, generous, and life-giving work, Laura Tremaine shows us how channeling her words into meaningful sharing changed her life—and how we can learn to do the same. Wise, warm, and relatable, this is the perfect read for anyone interested in exploring how to use their words to deepen their relationships.

Anne Bogel, author of *Don't Overthink It:*
Make Easier Decisions, Stop Second-Guessing,
and Bring More Joy to Your Life and host of
the *What Should I Read Next?* podcast

Listen, you need Laura Tremaine in your life. She has such a gift for the real, deep, life-changing sort of friendship that eludes so many of us. If female friendship has felt like a foreign land without a map, Laura is your best guide—funny, warm, knowledgeable, honest, relatable, and just the right sort of best-friend-bossy. She will guide you not only to deeper friendships with other women but to a deeper understanding and compassion for yourself. I love this book.

> **Sarah Bessey,** author of
> *Jesus Feminist* and *Miracles*
> *and Other Reasonable Things*

I've always loved Laura for her curiosity and for the way she pushes people into deeper conversations, whether it's on Instagram or her podcast or at a table of friends. While the details may be different, I think most people will recognize their own story in Laura's, as she stirs readers on to consider their own narratives on everything from faith to friendship to love and parenting. This is a book you're going to want your friends to read, one that will be a catalyst for amazing conversations.

> **Kristen Howerton,** author of
> *Rage Against the Minivan: Learning*
> *to Parent Without Perfection*

Laura Tremaine is a phenomenal storyteller, and her debut book is now officially one of my all-time favorites. Beyond Laura's honest vulnerability and graceful charm, the true gift of this book is the delightful alchemy that emerges at the end of every chapter where, after reading her story, I was compelled to share my own. Five stars! Three cheers! I adore this book.

> **Emily P. Freeman,** *Wall Street*
> *Journal* bestselling author of
> *The Next Right Thing*

As a self-proclaimed open book, even I had yet to go to the places Laura Tremaine leads us when it comes to opening up. I am forever changed by her words and her invitation to share my stuff. Tremaine knows there is more depth and richness to be had in our relationships and she graciously leads us by sharing her own raw, sometimes suspenseful, and tender stories. *Share Your Stuff. I'll Go First.* is a masterclass on how to open up, share with vulnerability and grace, and in return connect with those around us in ways we could never imagine.

Bri McKoy, author of *Come & Eat: A Celebration of Love and Grace Around the Everyday Table*

Laura is the consummate host and hand-holder as she invites you to share who you are, where you've been, and what you've experienced. But she does not ask you to be this vulnerable without going first. Laura opens each chapter with her own intimate stories of joy and triumph and loss and fear so we can see exactly how it's done. In *Share Your Stuff. I'll Go First.*, Laura gives us the manual to create connections with new and old friends, and most importantly, with ourselves.

Jamie Golden, cohost of *The Popcast with Knox and Jamie* and *The Bible Binge* podcasts

Share Your Stuff. I'll Go First.

10 Questions to Take Your Friendships to the Next Level

LAURA TREMAINE

ZONDERVAN BOOKS

ZONDERVAN BOOKS

Share Your Stuff. I'll Go First.
Copyright © 2021 by Laura Tremaine

Requests for information should be addressed to:
Zondervan, *3900 Sparks Dr. SE, Grand Rapids, Michigan 49546*

Zondervan titles may be purchased in bulk for educational, business,
fundraising, or sales promotional use. For information, please email
SpecialMarkets@Zondervan.com.

ISBN 978-0-310-35987-6 (audio)

Library of Congress Cataloging-in-Publication Data

Names: Tremaine, Laura, 1979- author.
Title: Share your stuff. I'll go first. : 10 questions to take your friendships
    to the next level / Laura Tremaine.
Description: Grand Rapids : Zondervan, 2021. | Summary: "Despite
    our hyper-connected culture, women are lonelier than ever and
    often shamed for being vulnerable. With intriguing storytelling and
    thoughtful questions, popular blogger and podcaster Laura Tremaine
    presents Share Your Stuff. I'll Go First., a guide to cultivating the
    authentic connection with others that only comes from sharing
    yourself"-- Provided by publisher.
Identifiers: LCCN 2020036114 (print) | LCCN 2020036115 (ebook) | ISBN
    9780310359852 (hardcover) | ISBN 9780310359869 (ebook)
Subjects: LCSH: Female friendship. | Vulnerability (Personality trait)
Classification: LCC BF575.F66 T77 2021 (print) | LCC BF575.F66 (ebook)
    | DDC 177/.62--dc23
LC record available at https://lccn.loc.gov/2020036114
LC ebook record available at https://lccn.loc.gov/2020036115

The names and identifying details of some individuals discussed in this book
have been changed to protect their privacy.

The author is represented by the literary agency of Alive Literary Agency,
www.aliveliterary.com.

Art direction: Curt Diepenhorst
Cover design: Faceout Studio | Spencer Fuller
Interior design: Kait Lamphere

Printed in the United States of America

20 21 22 23 24 25 26 27 28 /LSC/ 15 14 13 12 11 10 9 8 7 6 5 4 3 2 1

For Jeff. Who hears me despite all of my words.

And for Lucy and Finch.
May you never stop sharing.

Contents

Foreword

I met Laura Tremaine a few years ago, when our kids were attending the same local preschool. One day, our boys conspired to have a weekend playdate, and I found myself driving to the house of a person I'd never met, hoping I'd have something in common with the mom of my son's new friend.

When we arrived, we were greeted by a bright and chatty woman who welcomed us into her home and happily served us a giant bowl of queso and Fritos. Now, keep in mind, this is Los Angeles, the land of no carbs—no one serves Fritos and queso. In fact, you're lucky to get any kind of carb in this town. So I was super impressed when she confidently plopped down a bowl of processed cheese paired with a heaping pile of processed chips. I dug right in.

Our conversation began with the typical ice-breaking small talk, with Laura inquiring where I'm from. I responded that I hailed from St. Louis, Missouri. Now, in my experience, most conversations tend to stop there, unless the person I'm talking to has a personal connection to the city or a weird fascination with the St. Louis arch. But with Laura, there's no stopping. She simply paused and then said, "Tell me more about St. Louis."

What followed was a three-hour conversation about our journeys from our respective hometowns. I found myself discussing my hopes and dreams, motivations, successes and failures—all with someone I'd just met. Laura asks lots of questions. Yes, she's a very curious person, a voracious reader, and a constant seeker of information, but this compulsion to ask questions is about something deeper. She likes to facilitate connections, to probe and prod until she's discovered a place of deep, mutual understanding. I came away from my initial time spent with Laura feeling a deeper sense of connection. She possesses a rare gift.

Lucky for me, our boys became best friends, and we spent years hanging out together nearly every weekend, talking about anything and everything. One time, I marveled at her ability to read so many books, remarking that I'd finished maybe two novels since my kids had been born. I told her I'd tried book clubs (to be accountable), audiobooks (I never finished a single one), reading at night, reading in the morning, reading on vacation, but nothing worked. I still had piles of unfinished books I was deeply interested in reading. This question prompted Laura to explain in great detail how she organizes her morning routine and why. (It's the "and why" part that is uniquely Laura. Lots of people are willing to tell you their routine, but Laura is willing to go deeper.) She told me that she starts each day by setting a timer and reading a book, making herself read for twenty minutes, no interruptions allowed. In typical Laura fashion, the conversation didn't stop there. She went on to explain the guilt she felt about taking that space in the mornings, about the mental gymnastics she had to do to get herself to enjoy her time. Her honesty prompted me to admit that I also had a hard time taking space for things outside of work or childcare, that I wrestled with the expectations of motherhood and wondered where they came from. This conversation went on for hours. In the following days, I returned to this conversation again and again, reflecting on the questions it had inspired, allowing me to identify and break through many personal roadblocks when it came to my ability to practice self-care. On a side note, I tried Laura's trick of setting a timer, and since our conversation that day, I've read dozens and dozens of books.

In talking with Laura, I'm always challenged to go deeper, to uncover details I hadn't thought about in years. She doesn't want to hear my well-rehearsed "greatest hits" stories that are always impressive at dinner parties. She wants to hear the unrehearsed stories, the ones that have the strongest influence over me personally, the ones that are harder to share.

Share Your Stuff. I'll Go First. is the book version of spending an afternoon with Laura. In each chapter, she poses a seemingly simple question that will help guide you deeper into yourself. Then, through personal sharing, she shows you how to open up, staying with you every step of the way. Eventually, you will get to know Laura almost as intimately as you know yourself. After this initial step of self-discovery, Laura will encourage you to share what you've learned, to start a conversation with someone and open up about your experience. This step is a vital part of the lesson. In these current times of divisions, it's more important than ever to create intimate connections with others.

I'm lucky to have a friend like Laura, a friend who says, "Tell me more." Now, with this book, you will have the same friend, someone who shares first, who isn't afraid to look silly or say too much. *Share Your Stuff. I'll Go First.* is a safe place to start your journey toward deeper connections. So get out the Fritos, fire up a bowl of queso, and get started!

Jenna Fischer, actor, author, and producer/
cohost of the *Office Ladies* podcast

Introduction:
Share Your Stuff

n the earliest days of 2010, when online personal diaries of motherhood were all the rage, I launched a mommy blog. Mommy blogs had already peaked. I was, if anything, a little late to the game. No matter. Come one, come all, the internet said. There's a space for everyone.

Before I bought a domain name and slapped a website banner at the top, I had been reading personal blogs for a while. It was fascinating to watch people publish what were essentially their journal entries. I had been keeping a journal since I was child, scribbles full of angst and heartbreak that eventually morphed into more thoughtful and mature brooding. I couldn't fathom putting these pages up for the public to pore over, but that's exactly what bloggers were doing. With what felt like lightning speed, the internet had leveled the playing field for people to share their lives and opinions. The rise of everyday voices online was a beautiful thing.

The way people were sharing themselves in these blog posts left me breathless. I didn't know other women felt the same way I did about things—all kinds of things. I didn't know one could write so casually and yet be so compelling. Naturally, I wanted in on this action. There is a low bar of entry for writing on the internet, and it wasn't hard to find fellow mothers to read my Mommy Mondays feature on a blog I named *Hollywood Housewife*. This name was always meant to be tongue-in-cheek, though it was also literal. I had recently quit my longtime job in television production to start a family, and our home was located in Beachwood Canyon in Los Angeles, right underneath the Hollywood sign. I thought I was uniquely positioned for mommy blogging as the mom in a "normal" family in the entertainment industry. I was right. The blog gained an audience.

The harder truth, though, was that my desire to start blogging was born out of immense loneliness. From the outside, my personal life looked like a dream. I was happily married to my husband, Jeff, and we were proud parents of our first child, a baby girl. But even though it was the domestic life I wanted, I struggled with anxiety and panic, anger and sadness.

I didn't have any friends. Or rather, I did have friends—lifelong friends, actually—but they were hometown and college friends from Oklahoma, and they didn't know my life in LA. We tried phone dates and email, but we were all growing apart. In the years after college, I emailed back and forth daily with these friends, regaling them with stories about working on TV shows and the crazy nightlife in Hollywood. But as time marched on, and our mid-twenties became our late twenties, my childhood friends got entrenched in their own families and careers. I moved my private email stories to the public blog.

It wasn't that I didn't know anyone in Los Angeles. I met plenty of people doing the LA freelance hustle. Like me, they were from the middle of the country and not the coasts: Texas, Ohio, Illinois. We were all mostly eager to shake off our small town-ness and make it big. During my seven years of working at MTV, VH1, and Fox, I met dozens of people a lot like me. We could have been friends. But LA is tough that way.

When I started *Hollywood Housewife*, I ached for the type of girlfriends I'd known in Oklahoma. I wanted to be myself without name-dropping about who knew whom, what movies we'd worked on, which lists at which doors we could get on. I wanted baggy sweatpants and no-makeup girlfriends. I didn't want to be laughed at for the way I voted or what I thought about God (or that I thought about God at all). It seemed unbelievable to me that in a city of five million people, I couldn't find a friend group. I knew how to be a good friend. I knew all the rules. But the girlfriend code was different in California.

And so I took to the internet. People I'd never met in person became my closest confidants. Before social media, a big part of blogging was hanging out in the comments. The interaction was a huge draw online; it was still revolutionary that you could create a thing, share a thing, and get immediate feedback on that thing. As my blog grew, a few threads of thought stood out to me in the comments section. Most of the comments were from other bloggers, and they spilled their feelings into comment boxes that led back to their own blogs and wordy posts of their own. We were all furiously typing our hearts out into whatever blank white space awaited us.

It turned out my fellow bloggers were often lonely too. We just wanted to be heard, so we wrote and wrote and wrote. But then I started to hear from other readers, non-bloggers who read mommy blogs religiously. The messages from these women often began or ended with some sort of encouragement for me to keep sharing my life online, because while they loved my authenticity/transparency/honesty, they would never (ever) put themselves out there like that. They wanted me to keep sharing because they felt like they couldn't.

It took me a long time to see what *wasn't* being said in these comments and emails. Like me, these women were feeling disconnected, and they were unsure how to remedy it. They'd been taught it was tacky to talk about yourself and reckless to be vulnerable. They'd been told to stuff down their pain and focus only on the positive. But now they were starting to feel invisible in their jobs, in their marriages, in the grind of motherhood. They wondered if all this online chatter was making them feel better or worse.

As blogging became ubiquitous and social media started to explode, it was all too easy to judge those who shared their lives openly. Authenticity online became less a novelty and more likely to incite an eye roll. We branded oversharers as desperate, insecure, attention-seeking, or getting a little too big for their britches. (That's my Oklahoma childhood coming out.) As we witnessed the backlash to sharing ourselves, the slander and snark shut a lot of us right down, online and off. For women of a certain age, the fear of being maligned silenced us.

The hang-ups around sharing look something like this:

Will I look dumb?
Will I regret sharing?
What if I don't get my facts or thoughts stated exactly right?
Will someone use what I share against me?
*What if sharing makes me feel the feelings I've been
    actively pushing away for years?*

Well, frankly, all of that might happen, whether you share online or off.

I've felt all those complicated emotions, too. Even though I've spent nearly a decade talking about my life, my family, my mental health journey, and my general opinions on the internet, I still sometimes have mixed feelings about my transparency. I've said too much occasionally, things I regret and wish I could take back. Many, many times, I haven't said enough, not speaking up when I should have, choosing to keep the peace over facing conflict. Sharing too little is a regret that looms large. I convinced myself I was being smart and safe when I stayed quiet, but mostly I was being a coward.

I've learned better, over the years, what to share and with whom to share it. It is a delicate dance, learning to share in a way that is helpful and not harmful to the human spirit. We often learn our personal boundaries by misstep, saying too much and leaving a wound open for public consumption. So it's scary to think about sharing, on the chance that it might go awry.

But I believe it's worth the risk.

When I started blogging, an amazing thing happened. Sharing myself online and in person forced me to remember who I am at my core, because when I'm sharing, I can't hide. Staying present enough to verbally process or write out my feelings has kept me from living on autopilot.

As I began talking openly about my life online, I also began talking more openly offline. Sharing begat sharing, and I started having more satisfying and thoughtful conversations. I dropped the negative voice in my head that told me I wasn't worthy of good adult friendships. Sharing my stuff with friends—the silly stuff, the hard stuff—deepened all of my relationships. It has also held me accountable for ensuring my soul gets the life-giving connection it needs. Believe me when

I say learning to channel my words into meaningful sharing has changed my life.

Once I got into a rhythm of sharing myself with others, I also started journaling again. After a long season of that habit lying dormant, it cracked me wide open to see my own handwriting on a page, to see myself working through the emotions of my past and present. Journaling made me start paying attention to the details and patterns in my life. It turns out that sharing myself *with* myself was the most transformative of all. I want this discovery for you, too.

I have not always connected the dots between sharing and inner wholeness. I've gone through seasons of quiet. But as I've gotten older, as I've begun caring less about what people think and more about what brings me joy and peace, it's been undeniable that the sharing—the connecting—has been the magic elixir.

Listening

I can't talk about sharing your stuff without saying a word about listening. Sharing is a two-way street, and the listening portion is crucial. If you're someone who, like me, needs just the tiniest excuse to start talking, then I want to remind you—as I remind myself every day—to take time to stop and listen. Listen to what people are saying (or not saying). People will tell you exactly who they are if you listen closely.

Without a doubt, when I show up in my relationships as my whole self, without pretense; when I share my stuff with another human, online or off; I am better for it. Even when life is imperfect (and it's always imperfect). I have been lost and lonely, anxiety-ridden, bored, and needy, and sharing those feelings with a friend has almost always made me feel more human and less crazy. I have been full of joy, on top of the world, and bursting with happiness, and sharing it with someone I love has almost always enhanced the moment. When I try to shut down my feelings—the good and the bad—that's when I feel isolated. That's when I swirl with self-doubt.

So I don't shut down so much anymore. I've learned that sharing our stuff is the key to connection and consciousness.

• • •

Years after I gave up mommy blogging, I decided to start a new online hub focused on all the things we have to share. I called it *10 Things to Tell You*, and emphasized that YOU have 10 Things to Tell. We all do, but many of us don't know how to share our stuff. So each week on the *10 Things to Tell You* podcast, I provide a prompt and encourage listeners to take that topic to their best friend, their partner, or their journal. The prompt is a conversation starter. It's a place to begin to talk more deeply with one another.

This book follows a similar format. Each chapter poses one of life's big questions for you to ponder, followed by my own answer in essay form. Let it be known that I am no expert. I picked these topics myself, based on ten years of sharing and listening online, and on thousands of hours of conversations with friends about the milestones of our lives. I hope these 10 questions make you think about your life. I hope the stories make you think about the moments and the people who have had the greatest impact on your journey. I want these chapters to help you identify these things and then share them with someone you trust.

You don't need to read this book the way you normally would, from start to finish. You *can* read it that way, of course. Or, you can simply browse the chapter titles and jump around to the topics that interest you most. The lists of 10 between chapters are meant to break up the questions, which can make you feel quite vulnerable, and give you an idea for the variety of things you can share about yourself or ask for in others.

I envision you reading this book by sharing it with a best friend or a partner or with your group of girlfriends over margaritas, going through the chapters together and answering them from a place of truth. The things you've never talked about as well as the stories you've trotted out so many times you've memorized the punch lines.

Let these questions spark conversations. Sharing is contagious, so I'm hopeful that sharing my stuff will lead you to share yours. Our time on earth is short, and building connections with one another makes every season better.

I want you to share your stuff. I'll go first.

Chapter
ONE

Who Are You?

Let's just start at the very beginning, shall we?

Who are you?

What's the first thing that springs to mind when you're asked that question? Your name? Your family? Your hometown? Your profession? Your habits or hobbies? Does your first thought revolve around your relationship to others—you're a parent, a friend, a spouse, an employee?

This question addresses our most basic identity, whatever we consider that to be. My core identity includes a few choices that were made for me—where I grew up, how many siblings I have—and many choices around the life I've created now: where I live, my family roles, my personal values and beliefs. It also includes some intangibles, such as my preferences and my personality. There are a handful of things that are so crucial to my story and how I see myself that nothing else is worth telling until you know these pieces.

I understand if this question is overwhelming, right here at the outset. Often, when I ask someone who they are, and they can see that I mean it genuinely, a look of panic will cross their face. It's like we have a fleeting moment of uncertainty, I mean, WHO AM I, anyway? Maybe I don't want to tell you. I'm not *sure I trust you really want to know. How much time do you have? How deep should we go?*

Let's not overthink it, though. By the end of this book, you'll have laid out your most important moments and turning points. Right now, just think of the first five things that make you YOU. Remember, there's never a wrong answer here. We're on a quest for introspection and connection, and we have to start somewhere.

So who am I?

Well, I'm glad you asked.

I'll Go First

My name is Laura, and I pull my hair out.

I have so much anxiety that it comes out in involuntary self-harm. That's the first thing I want you to know about me because it takes any doubt about my weirdness off the table.

I've always been a hair puller. I started pulling my hair out at the roots sometime during the toddler stage. It's a coping mechanism that feels like part of me, evidence of my messy mind right there on display on my messy head, from as far back as I can remember. Why would anyone choose to pull out her hair, causing her to have bald spots and broken follicles? Because it's a soothing, repetitive motion, that's why; it calms me to feel the tug and then hear the rip. It's a faint sound, but I'm attuned to it.

When it suddenly became "brave" to talk about mental health struggles, I got very chatty about my lifelong anxiety and the existential fear I feel in my bones every single day. It doesn't bother me to tell you about any of it. I have always separated my mental health from my self-worth; I've never viewed it as something to be ashamed of. My fear, my hair pulling—these things are facts about me, the same as telling you where I went to college or my eye color. My lack of pretense around it comes, I suspect, from my parents. They acted like my anxiety was just a part of my personality. It wasn't embarrassing. It wasn't something to be treated, either. It just was. *Little Laura worries a lot.*

And it's true that I have always been afraid of something. I am scared all the time that someone is going to die, that there's going to be a loud noise, that I'll be found out as a fraud, that I did something bad or wrong and I just don't know it yet, but someone is going to let me know in a really awful way any minute now.

And then, when someone does die, or I do something bad or wrong, I do not then think that the worst has passed. Sometimes, depending on the weight of the situation, I don't even let it sink in that this thing I've been thinking about has now happened. Instead, my mind simply leapfrogs over the moment and the cycle of fear starts again. Because someone is gonna die, there's about to be a loud noise, and I frequently do something bad or wrong, even if by accident.

So that's why I'm telling you about this first, the hair pulling. I like to lead with this information. It tells the other person exactly the level of anxiety they're dealing with, and then I don't have to apologize for my unfounded fears later.

•   •   •

My name is Laura, and I grew up in Oklahoma, but I live in California now. These two facts are central to who I am.

My parents and my two older siblings were also raised in Oklahoma, and they all still live there. Even more than the hair pulling, this happenstance of my birthplace informs much of my identity.

In the early 1970s, my parents moved to a teeny, one-stoplight town just a few miles north of the Texas border. By the time I was born, my sister, Dawn, was nine and my brother, Lance, was seven. My tumultuous and near-fatal entrance into this world ensured that there would be no more children after me. The age gap between me and the older two meant that we have entirely different memories of what our parents were like and the culture of our childhood home. My brother and sister were both out of the house before I turned ten, so I lived in the hybrid space of having older siblings but being treated in many ways as an only child.

Life in Oklahoma is not what you might expect. Outsiders have visions of horses and teepees and dusty plains and tornadoes and football. And Oklahoma has all of those things, along with a murky history, but these stereotypes don't do the people of Oklahoma justice. Oklahomans are—to make my own generalizations—generous and kind. They work hard and care deeply. It's like anywhere, I guess. When a place is your home, you know it better than anyone, but you also can't see it objectively.

I feel differently about Oklahoma now than I did growing up, when it felt like the middle of Nowheresville with no way out, flat land stretching hundreds of miles in every direction between small towns. I feel differently about Oklahoma now than I did when I was in high school and the bombing of the Alfred P. Murrah Federal Building in Oklahoma City showed the world how resourceful and resilient the state could be. I feel differently about Oklahoma now than I did when I first moved to California and was forced to defend it daily from ignorant people mocking the middle of the country as ignorant. I feel differently about Oklahoma now than I did when I decided never to move back.

But no matter what phase I'm in, Oklahoma was my first home and the first place that shaped me. Growing up there gave me a sensibility I will never quite shake: it's kept me grounded in reason and reality. I was raised among farmers and rodeos and spent my entire childhood two hours from the nearest airport. My biggest rebellion was sneaking out to climb into the back of somebody's pickup truck, going 100 mph on old country roads, and meetin' up at the drive-in next to the bowling alley. I'm nostalgic for somewhere that sounds a lot like a country music song, and if you stick around long enough, you'll hear an accent that reveals it all.

I'd made my life in California for more than ten years before I stopped answering the casual question, "Where are you from?" with a proud, "Oklahoma, but I live in Los Angeles." Most people asking this question want to know where you lay your head at night, but I always took the question more literally. It felt important to me that others should know I didn't grow up in California. I wasn't a West Coast-er by nature. Oklahoma was where I started. That red dirt will always be a part of me.

But I *chose* Los Angeles. I moved here sight unseen when I was twenty-two years old, and I felt like an outsider for a long time. Slowly, LA became home and let me spread my wings in anonymity. I grew accustomed to the weather and the attitude and the lifestyle—that particular blend of glamour and hippie-dippie and urban and relaxed neuroses. Los Angeles is a city full of seekers, and that feels right for me.

So these two places I call home go hand-in-hand, and if

you're getting to know me, I will likely talk about both of them in the first five minutes. I left my small town on purpose, and I've made my life in Los Angeles. One place is a foundation; the other means freedom. These two places have become part of my identity.

• • •

My name is Laura, and I am a daughter.

When I was five or six, I remember looking through an old, disintegrating photo album. I was at my grandparents' house, sitting cross-legged on the peeling hardwood floor, turning the fragile, plastic-covered pages carefully with my little hands. My parents didn't care much about memory keeping, and there weren't a lot of family photos in albums or on the walls. My mom kept a single dresser drawer of some of her favorites. When I was at Granny and Pappy's house, where they had photos and keepsakes on display, I would pore over them, searching for clues about where I came from and how it related to who I was becoming.

I came across an old group photo from a large family gathering—it looked like a reunion or maybe a holiday. It had been taken out in the driveway and loved ones were staged in row after row. I zeroed in immediately on the seated first row, where a little girl with stringy bangs sat perched on the knee of an elder. She had on a red plaid jumper and wore a shy, crooked smirk in place of a smile.

I brought the photo to my mom. "I don't remember taking this picture," I said. I was a little indignant, already suspecting on some level that my identity had been stolen from me in this snapshot.

Mom looked at me in surprise, then amusement. "That's

me," she said. "I'm a little girl here, sitting on Pappy's lap. I think I'm a little younger here than you are now."

"It can't be," I said, peering closer. The rest of the photo became clearer then, how the colors looked surreal, the clothes and hairstyles old-fashioned. But I hadn't noticed any of that at first because of my certainty that I was the one in the photo. I stared hard at the yellowed paper, now with the knowledge that it was my mom, not me, captured in a moment more than thirty-five years before. I couldn't separate my own face from the one staring back at me. I saw myself in every part of it, even the posture and the placement of her hands. I was her, and she was me.

I didn't feel time collapse again like that until I became a mom another twenty-five years later, when in my body and smells and movements, I was constantly aware of my both my new baby and my own mother, who then lived thousands of miles away. The scent of my motherhood—breast milk and sweat and breath—clung to me all day and through the sleepless nights. I didn't so much feel as though I was turning into my mother; it was more that I felt I had always *been* her, from that 1950s photograph to 2010, and nothing that had happened in between mattered. It was enough to make me believe in reincarnation if we hadn't both still been living.

For better or worse, we are all products of our parents in some way. We have no choice in the DNA that threads through us, and it can be a source of pride, frustration, privilege, or just cold, hard facts. Genetics gave me my mother's face and my father's smile. But what if you don't know how science played out in your bodily features, in your health, or in your personality? What if you can't confidently debate nature versus nurture because the nurture part can be parsed, but the nature element is a mystery?

My dad was abandoned in the hospital at birth in 1943. Fifty-five years later, we met his biological mom together, in awe of what time and genetics can do.

When I was growing up, Dad barely uttered a word about this childhood or his parents. Any information I gleaned came from my mom, who repeated the few stories she knew. Dad had been raised out in the woods of Shawnee, Oklahoma, without running water. His dad was illiterate; his mother was tough. They brought their surprise son home from the hospital wrapped in newspaper. My sweet-natured, resilient father, who everyone understands within moments of meeting him is highly intelligent, stood out in his small adoptive family but was never told the circumstances of his birth. He discovered his biological differences in a high school class where they were studying blood types. The science of his type coming from theirs was impossible. The loving parents who raised him died shortly after, from hardship and illness. They never knew he had uncovered their secret.

This story was not something we talked about in our family. Dad went on to put himself through college, then law school. He married my mom, became an officer in the Air Force, went into private practice, and had three lovely children. The details of how he got through all that were lost to me, but the takeaways—the bootstraps, the independence— those are what our family belief system is built on. No one ever made the outright connection for me that where a person comes from—what womb, what DNA courses through their veins—has anything to do with who they are.

Still, I wondered. Starting early, I bypassed seeing the

Dad who was standing in front of me in favor of daydreaming about who he (we) would be if he hadn't been adopted. My young imagination made up elaborate stories about his birth mom. Was she a famous movie star? Maybe she was royalty? My dad is quite regal. Anyone who has ever known him can see that he possesses something special, something other-worldly. He expects good manners, and he holds your gaze with his sparkly blue eyes just a beat too long. He is formal and exacting. Growing up, my friends teased me when they called our house, because Dad always answered the phone with a baritone "Good evening," instead of a traditional hello. I decided he had surely inherited all of this from his birth parents. His mother must have been beautiful. Noble in her choice to give up her beloved baby. Whatever was so special about her would have been passed down to him, and then, of course, to me. Dad's unknown lineage left a lot of possibility for me when I considered the question, *Who am I?*

And then, when I was a freshman at the University of Oklahoma, sleeping in a 10 x 10 dorm room, sorority insignias covering every square inch, I took a phone call at the end of the hall. My sister Dawn, by then a lawyer and a new mom, had found our father's biological mother in Enid, a town about an hour north of the dingy campus rec room.

I stood frozen on the pilling blue carpet while my sister spoke slowly, describing how she'd called the woman she believed to be our grandmother and hung up twice before having the courage to speak to her. The old voice on the other end of Dawn's phone call had been quiet before admitting that giving up her baby was something she "hadn't thought about in a long time."

This woman, who had carried my father in her womb for

9

the better part of a year, was a real person and not a fantasy. Moreover, she didn't appear to have mystical powers. In fact, she was an Oklahoman like we were, living not far from where Dad grew up. It was all very disorienting.

Our family met Dot, my biological grandmother, a few months later at my sister's home, less than a hundred miles from where Dot had lived all eighty years of her life. On the appointed day, she came up the driveway slowly. But when she saw our family assembled there in the living room, wide-eyed and slack-jawed, her face broke into an expression of open delight. Her spirit, sparkle, and smile were an exact replica of my father's.

In those first breathtaking moments, no one knew what to do with their hands or their eyes. I tried not to stare, but the resemblance between my dad and his biological mother was undeniable. Dot herself was overcome, laughing and singing a little. She was loud, her bold presence filled the space, and I was so surprised by this. Until that moment, I didn't know that I expected her to be quiet and contemplative while meeting the child she never knew. I anticipated that she had carried a burden all these years. Instead, she was obviously filled with joy—with herself, with the family she'd just met, and with the unusual situation in which we were all now engaged, flustered, witnessing a full range of emotions on the face of everyone in the room. My biological grandmother was nervous but exuberant. I was shocked by such an overt display of emotion. She shared the mannerisms and facial features of my father, but she wasn't restrained like he was, and like I had been taught to be. She wore all of her big feelings on the outside. A part of me whispered, "There you are." Dot wasn't magical, but she was instantly familiar. I felt a pull that I wanted to resist. Sitting on my sister's couch, unknown to us just weeks before, was an explanation for my personality.

Meeting Dot came with a tidal wave of understanding, but it wasn't the lesson about identity I would have predicted. By the time I was eighteen, watching that reunion of mother and son, I had (mostly) dropped the royal lineage fantasies, but I had begun to assume that through my blood ran rebellion or maybe shame. I wondered if there was a direct tie to my soul of whatever secret possessed a woman to abandon a baby at the hospital, without arrangements or even proper paperwork.

But not only was Dot not a princess, she was also not a cautionary tale. Dot came from a loving, middle-class, educated family. She had been quite progressive for the time when my father was conceived in the 1940s, living with friends, working in a salon and owning her own car. She told us about that time in her life with fondness in her voice. She went on to have a long marriage and many wonderful relationships in her community and church. We learned quickly that Dot was universally loved. My dad has a similar magnetism, but he grew up in poverty and without examples of joy and liveliness. Meeting Dot changed the way I viewed my dad and, in turn, the way I viewed myself, because where there had been a missing piece there was now a human being. I didn't have to wonder what a long-lost grandmother might be like; she was there in front of me, with her beauty, her flaws, her choices, and a demeanor that had carried through to the next two generations. And yet the biology wasn't without a dash of magic.

A year or two after we first met, during a time of cautious relationship, I drove with my parents and sister up to Dot's home in Enid. During the visit, we were all sitting and chatting in the small living room when the trill of the phone cut the niceties. It was extra loud, the ringing, and Dot labored from her chair to the entry table. We lapsed into polite silence as she lifted the receiver toward her ear.

"Good afternoon," she crowed into the phone.

Collectively, every jaw on the faux velvet couch dropped open. Never in my life before or since have I heard another human being answer their home phone in this manner. Except for, of course, my dad, who had always eschewed the functional "Hello" and instead referenced the time of day in his formal answer to a ring.

Good morning.

Good afternoon.

Good evening.

When Dot answered the phone in this same, ridiculous manner, all the magic of my father's biological roots showed themselves. It was deeper than eye color. It was more than learned traits. Both Dad and Dot had a preference toward formality that came out in learned phrases they couldn't possibly have picked up from one another. They shared something indefinable in their spirit.

The idea that we're in full control of our identities is an illusion. Yes, we can forge our own way. We can commit to rewriting a biological story that has defined a family for too long. But our DNA makes many defining choices about who we are. We cannot escape it. When I share that being a daughter is one of the most important aspects of who I am, it's not because of the outward-facing relationship I maintain with my parents, although at forty years old and with half a continent between us, I'm proud that we remain close.

What matters to me now about being a daughter is that so much of my adulthood—and now, my motherhood—points back to my family of origin. Much of what I believe about myself today comes from who my parents told me I was when I was young. They told me I was the luckiest girl in the world to be born in America, in Oklahoma, in my exact family. They whole-heartedly believed I was the smartest kid in the class and entirely capable of independence, so I believed I was smart, capable, and independent. They set me up for success, and it worked. Whatever they felt about my hair pulling and the fearful nature that led to migraines and panic, they taught me to swim in the world by dumping me in the deep end of the ocean. They waved and said they'd see me on the other side when I got there. I got the message early that I had to figure it all out on my own or die trying. My fears, my bald spots, my life path.

●　●　●

My name is Laura, and I am a mother.

My daughter, Lucy Jane Tremaine, tore into the world on a Sunday evening in October 2009. The trauma I sustained during her birth, resulting in a blood transfusion and what felt like a permanent rearrangement of my lower organs, was overshadowed by how much my husband Jeff and I loved this dark-haired, grumpy-faced baby. She was perfect. I told the nurses that I felt nothing but pity for the other moms on my floor, who had to compare their own body's offerings to that of my beautiful girl, who was looking suspiciously around the nursery.

Lucy was just weeks old when I first asked Jeff if he thought the baby knew I was her mom. Jeff is an artist, but he is profoundly logical, with Viking ancestors and a military surgeon father. He looked at me, naturally, like my question was bonkers.

"Of course she knows you're her mom. Who else would you be?" He kept his eyes above my chin, and they did not drift down to the breastmilk stains on the shirt I'd been wearing for several days.

But I wasn't so sure. I stared down at little Lucy but didn't feel overcome with the protective mama bear instinct. I got no spiritual signals that she knew she was part of me.

I started asking Jeff the question nightly, and with increasing desperation.

"Do you think she knows I'm her mom?"

He was patient at first, knowing not to get exasperated with my incessant questioning and over analysis. He listed all the ways mother and child *know* one another in the deepest sense. He cited scientifically studied animal behavior. He saw the franticness in my eyes and tried to calm this newfound fear, that seemed to have come out of nowhere and was slightly nonsensical.

Eventually, though, he resorted to answering in jokes.

"That baby has no idea who you are," he'd deadpan. "In fact, she whispered to me this morning, 'Who is this strange lady in the house all the time?'"

I worried that Lucy would mistake the babysitter for her mom, or think my own mom—who was visiting quite a bit— was her true mother. It didn't help that Lucy appeared to share a few personality traits with her dad—inheriting, it seemed, an innate confidence and reliance on no one. We teased that it was Lucy's world and we were all just living in it, that's how unaffected she was by anyone holding her, but secretly, I couldn't get a read on it. I didn't know if I felt like a mother should—if I felt like I was Lucy's mother, in a deep way, the way everyone describes—and I definitely couldn't tell if she favored me above anyone else.

So every night I asked Jeff if he thought Lucy knew I was her mom. It became a habit, like saying *goodnight* and *I love you*. It was a call and response between us, my fear laid bare on the pillow, and his assurance or sarcasm letting me feel heard regardless of his actual answer.

When Lucy was about nine months old, I was staring at her in a baby music class when love seemed to fall from the ceiling like an avalanche. My postpartum fog had recently lifted, and when the primal love arrived months later than imagined and at a strangely inopportune moment, I was overcome with feeling. I was someone's mother.

When our son, Finch, was born two years later, the questions resumed and turned from singular to plural.

"Do you think the kids know I'm their mom?"

I asked this every night, and every night Jeff responded.

The months flew by; the children grew. In turn, they learned to talk and called me *Mommy*. I loved the kids deeply, but it didn't feel how I thought it would. My anxiety kept me from experiencing peacefulness in our roles as mother and child. For years, I second-guessed myself and them because no one could tell me with certainty what this connection was really supposed to be. I worried I was missing a page in the parenting playbook.

My children were born close enough to one another that it felt like our house was in the "baby years" for a long time. Mommy culture warned me not to lose myself in motherhood, but try as I might, I did get a little lost there for a while. I wish those messages weren't wrapped in caution tape, but instead in the reassurance that women will, in fact, emerge from the woods. Because every single mom I know gets lost for a little bit, and then is found.

For a long time I fought not to include "mom" on my identity resume. My babies felt like the least interesting thing about me, even as I built an online presence about our family. I loved my children, of course, but I fully bought into the idea that I shouldn't define myself around motherhood, so I worked overtime to show everyone how independent I remained.

Except I wasn't the same person as I was before Lucy was born. Life forces your hand that way. Bringing up children, caring for them day after day, watching them become people, keeping careful tabs on the light in their eyes, I have succumbed to this intoxicating love. You couldn't possibly know me without seeing me raise Lucy and Finch.

I was a daughter, and now I'm a mother. The cycle continues. These things are half of who I am.

• • •

As a young person, I ruminated on the *Who am I?* question. It felt like the only question worth asking as I navigated childhood in Oklahoma, and it was a driving force in creating my own future when I moved to California. Now solidly in midlife, I still ask myself, *Who am I?* when I'm having trouble making a decision or when I need to find my footing in an ever-changing landscape. And I can return to the parts of my biology that I embrace, the choices I've made in an effort to live a life I'm proud of, and the series of random, meaningful preferences that make up my taste: a passion for Stephen King novels, bold lipstick, Dr. Pepper, and our pink living room walls.

The big things, the little things, all of it together makes up the whole of who I am, and outlining it clearly makes me feel like I am really here, on earth, and that my birth and my parents and my path and my children were not an accident.

I have a thousand things I could rattle off as something I think of as "me," but only a few are unchanging, the very core of my soul. I always come back to how I picture myself—not a city-living mother of two, but as a scrawny little girl, barefoot in the dusty Oklahoma sun, a ponytail covering the bald spots, a book in my hand, and big feelings just seconds from spilling out of my mouth. That's the woman calmly writing these words in Los Angeles. That's who I am.

Who are you?

Your Turn

When I ask you who you are, I'm not looking for the deepest, most eloquent response. I'm just asking how you see yourself. I'm asking where you're from, what your family looks like, what you're passionate about. What would you want people to know if you were going to be friends? Think of maybe three to five things that shape the way you move through the world.

Imagine that we're new friends, on a coffee date or maybe out for drinks. The restaurant's good, the vibe is relaxing. The potential for a fun and lasting friendship is in the air. Maybe this scenario makes you a little skittish, because you've been burned before by friends you trusted, friends who also "got" you. You don't want that to happen, but you're desperate for connection. So let's assume our friendship is the good kind. We're not going to break one another's hearts in a thousand ways over the years. We're going to hold steady, laugh a lot, extend all kinds of grace, and carry one another through. Mostly, we are going to talk and listen. We are each going to share our stories, however messy or perfectly crafted they are.

A few questions to get you started:

Where did you grow up?

Who were your heroes when you were young?

What were your family rules?

When did you first feel truly independent?

Does your life look now how you imagined?

If you could have any job in the world—regardless of
salary or hours or location—what would it be?

What's your most important relationship?

What do you do for fun?

Is there a problem area in your life that you wish you
could fix with the wave of a wand?

What is your greatest joy?

Take these questions and use one or two as prompts with a new or old friend the next time you're together. Pose the question and then go first. I think you'll be surprised by what you learn about one another, or where the conversation goes from there.

It's very telling to see how people answer this first question. Do they start with their family or their job? Do they point to a personality type? Do they lead with a defining event? Do they make a joke to ease the tension of the ultimate existential question: Who are you? Pay attention to how people respond. Pay attention to how YOU answer.

Weird Things I've Done

1. Set up shop at summer camp as "Bonita the Body Brusher" when I was twelve years old. I used a hairbrush on sunburned legs and shoulders as a means of resourceful exfoliation, and offered my services during the rest hour and charged dessert at the next meal. (After I reached adulthood, someone pointed out to me the benefits of the century-old practice of dry brushing. We just thought it felt good to brush our parched skin.)

2. Became a singing telegram for Valentine's Day. As part of a show-choir fundraising effort, I drove all over town with a boombox, delivering song and dance numbers for unsuspecting love birds.

3. Called the cops in high school when someone kept delivering pieces of junkyard furniture to my house and arranging them in little vignettes in the front yard. I was thoroughly freaked out by these random appearances of couches and recliners, some of which had smiley faces scratched into the faux leather, which I took as especially menacing. I blogged about the incident decades later, and a hometown friend let the truth slip out that the culprit was the same person I kept calling to come and help me remove the pieces. I think I'm still mad about it.

4. Sang my senior choir solo as a duet (the first weird part) and dedicated it to a boy in the audience (the more mortifying part).

5. Took a train from Oxford to London the day the fourth Harry Potter book was released, just to be in the city of the book's origin. I was delighted to see that all over London, people wore costumes and had drawn lightning bolts on their foreheads in celebration of the much-anticipated novel.

6. Followed Drew Barrymore out an open window onto a balcony at a holiday party just three months after I'd moved to Los Angeles. I chickened out and didn't talk to her, but I remember thinking I'd never seen a more beautiful person.

7. Answered the phone "Doggy Fizzle Televizzle" with a straight face during the time I worked on Snoop Dogg's television show for MTV.

8. Slept on the ground on the side of a cliff wearing a beaded dress and wrapped in a tablecloth during a coastal wedding that got quarantined after a terrible fire closed all the roads. Guests were stuck at the outdoor venue until the next morning.

9. Attended every single day of the murder trial for an extended family member, and interviewed the district attorney and multiple jurors on camera after the acquittal of the accused. I thought I wanted to be a documentarian, but after that, I realized I didn't have the stomach for it.

10. Defied the explicit instructions at a Judy Blume book signing not to gush over the author and took the few seconds allotted me to tell Ms. Blume that her work had changed my life. She smiled indulgently.

Chapter

TWO

Who Was There?

Some people see you through all the seasons of your life. They know you as one self, and then as the next self. They've seen you at your best and worst. Somehow, they are in the background of every story.

Then there are the people who make a short but lasting appearance. Maybe you only know them for a specific period of time, and their presence can never be lifted from that moment. Your interactions with them moved the plot forward. If your life was a movie, they would be nominated for a guest appearance.

The question Who Was There? is about identifying who was standing beside you when you got that life-changing phone call. Who introduced you to the person who became your roommate, or your spouse, or your boss? Who was your childhood best friend, your college sweetheart, the coworker at your first job, your neighbor when The Big Thing happened?

Their faces look out at you from old snapshots in weathered photo albums. Maybe sometimes you have to pause and think hard to remember their last names. Maybe not. Maybe you will never, ever, ever forget the details of who was there when.

For me, here, the answer to this question is a summer camp

friend, a first love, a helpful acquaintance, and a seatmate on an airplane.

I'll Go First

I'll start with Alli. She always seems to come up in my favorite childhood stories, even though she exited my life when I was seventeen and exited the world just last year.

Alli and I met at summer camp in Missouri when we were both turning eight years old. I know we were both turning eight because we shared a birthday week, and that week fell during our camp term. We were away from our families for a month in the mountains, without contact except for the occasional letter from home. Since camp cabins were sorted by birthday, we were fated to be together every June.

Alli and I had nothing in common. Even our astrological signs split us between Gemini and Cancer. I was growing up in a town of 3,500 in Oklahoma, in an extremely conservative family, and I was bookish and four-eyed with permed hair full of hidden tangles.

Alli was being raised by a single mom in the suburbs of Kansas City. She was funny and loud and unafraid of authority. She was cool with her trendy city clothes and pop culture references. Alli created nicknames and inside jokes in seconds, and her wit was quicker than that of any other kid I knew. She landed a punch line like she was on a sitcom.

In me, Alli found an eager audience. I've always been a sucker for someone who makes me laugh. The summer I met her, nothing seemed all that funny. New to camp, I was homesick and uncomfortable in my own skin, so much so that I faked a sprained ankle so I wouldn't have to participate in many of the camp's sporty activities. I'd just finished the second grade, where I'd had a cruel teacher and few friends. I was anxious and afraid my parents were going to die any moment (because that was how my brain worked). I'd pulled out enough of my hair to create three bald spots.

So when Alli swaggered into the cabin with her grand arm motions and made-up-on-the-spot chants and big laughter, the summer suddenly got three shades brighter. Discovering that we would both have birthdays during our time at camp took the sting out of the particular loneliness of being a kid away from family and school friends on her big day. Alli's mom sent a huge care package with goodies for the whole cabin, and Alli acted like having a camp birthday was a privilege instead of a scheduling oversight. Her easy attitude bled over into mine. Every year for the next eight years, we celebrated our birthday milestones together: turning ten, turning thirteen, "toasting" with fruit punch to sweet sixteen.

Since this was before the invention of the World Wide Web, Alli and I didn't communicate much during the eleven months when we weren't at camp. Every summer, we met up on the first day in our shared cabin, and each took stock of how the other had changed. Our belief systems morphed and our bodies matured, not incrementally but by leaps and bounds. We were children, then pre-pubescent, then teenagers. It was more than just symbolic that we showed up in every single birthday photo together for all those years; it was tradition. Here we are, growing up, changing ages, each acting as stand-ins for the family who wasn't there.

For both of us, these summers were an anomaly to the rest of our lives. Camp was full of zealous activity and rah-rah Jesus. We would canoe twenty miles and then pitch tents before attending a church service. We played kickball and learned to use a bow and arrow and prayed before and after every meal and game. We didn't have to impress anyone or escape anything, and we loved every second. After that first year, my anxiety when I was at camp was always at its lowest, and any drama from Alli's city life disappeared. This wasn't the summer camp of the after-school specials—we didn't sneak cigarettes or meet boys at midnight. Our contraband was candy that we hid in stuffed animals. At camp, we could be innocent and unafraid. We made millions of memories, some that became legendary in our minds. We played pranks on our counselors and won cabin competitions. Alli is in the foreground of every single one of my camp stories.

The year we both turned eighteen, I stood in the center of the cabin on the first day of camp and stared at the list of occupants in disbelief. Alli's name wasn't there. I ran next door, on the off chance that we had been separated for the first time in ten years. I scanned the list of names with my heart sinking. Her name wasn't there, either. Alli wasn't coming. We would both become legal adults in two weeks' time, but we wouldn't be together. A birthday apart for the first time since we were eight years old. Who would sing me the birthday song with such gusto? Whose hand would I squeeze to hold back the homesick tears?

I went to college and subsequently lost touch with Alli. When Google became a thing, I searched for her every six months or so. Already, she felt like a relic of childhood, but she was one I didn't want to lose. I thought of her often and hoped she was doing well. I wondered how life was turning out for her. With each new social media platform, I typed her name in the search bar, but it was always fruitless.

Finally, years after the birth of Facebook and well into family life, a late-night search led me to a profile that looked like it could actually be the summer camp Alli I'd been missing for so long. I sent her a message and held my breath. Had the years been kind to her memory? Did she hold me in the same regard that I'd held her in my childhood narrative?

The Alli I'd found was the right one. She accepted my friend request but was shy in her response. I scrolled her Facebook posts and sometimes hit "like" or made an emoji comment, but mostly, we kept a respectful distance. Our lives had turned out so differently. It wasn't surprising, really, but our relationship couldn't seem to make the leap to adulthood. Neither of us felt comfortable enough to broach a real conversation.

If we could just see each other in person, I thought, I would ask her all the questions that burned inside me, and I know we would have laughed about all our summer camp antics. I wanted to know how she felt about things now, all these years later. I wanted to know if she remembered us the way I remembered us. I thought I'd see her again. I really believed there was a reunion on the horizon. Our fortieth birthdays were coming up, and I was getting nostalgic about everything. I guessed that she was, too.

In the months before our next shared birthday milestone, I was online on a rainy spring afternoon when I saw that a stranger had tagged Alli with a line of crying emojis. I clicked on her profile, and at the top were multiple messages expressing grief.

I sat up in shock.

Alli died from complications of an elective surgery. Aside from a sappy blog post I wrote before we reconnected online, I never told her outright how much it meant to me that she was a constant presence in my life every summer of my childhood. I never told her that she colors every thought I have about celebrating birthdays.

My regret for not spelling that out to her was immediate, and I cried for a surprising number of days over a friend I hadn't seen in over twenty years. But when Alli died, the last vestige of my childhood slipped away. You don't realize how hard you hang onto the people and the memories that shaped you until suddenly, they're gone. Childhood friends hold such a tender place in our hearts. I couldn't have predicted the grief her death would bring, the sense of finality.

Alli was the witness to my growing up. We had lots of friends, counselors, the usual hubbub of kid activities at a sleepaway camp. But across crowded dining halls, we would lock eyes. In prayer circles, we'd find each other's hands. We could be wordless and then burst into peals of laughter. Our friendship transcended the circumstances. She was there, and I was there, and it mattered.

● ● ●

Clint Burns was my first kiss. I was in eighth grade, and he was my best friend from church.

That kiss was just how every love song says it's gonna be: perfect. We were in a concrete tunnel in a nearly empty sports stadium. Our mouths fit together just right, our bodies responded appropriately, and the proverbial fireworks appeared over our heads. I had many first kisses after that one, and they were far more awkward, confused, and bumpy.

Clint and I went to the same middle school, but were in different grades and different social circles. He was a jock. I was the editor of the yearbook. We shared a sense of humor and a reverence for our religion. In a community where youth group was the social event of the week, our little Bible church was not the happening place to be. We didn't have the flashy graphics, harmonizing worship teams, or exciting field trips of the Baptists. Nor did we have the cool factor of the Methodists. Our independent, charismatic church was out toward the edge of town, and though there were some prominent society members among our elders, we were considered kinda fringe. The parishioners at Cross of Christ raised their hands to Jesus during the worship time and prayed over you in tongues if you requested it.

I attended church on my own; my parents were not religious. I wore it as a symbol of my righteousness that I had chosen my faith, that I hadn't been drafted into it by my family. My parents agreed to drive me anywhere I wanted on Sunday mornings, and I chose the Bible church. This was proof that I was very holy.

Clint was already a rising football star in a town where sports was the ultimate currency. I could see his trajectory, and I thought my brains would make us a real team. An adolescent power couple, if you will.

He was my boyfriend as my body literally developed into womanhood. I felt confident and beautiful in his gaze. I thought we would be together forever.

Reader, I did not marry him.

Of course I didn't! I was fourteen years old! But maybe everyone thinks—at least for a minute—that they might spend the rest of their life with their first love. It's impossible to grasp that a person who means so much to you will turn out to be so temporary. A flash, really. A lightning bolt of a flash, maybe, in its importance, but still, as quick as that, it's over. My teenage self loved Clint with every cell of my being, and when he broke my heart, everything stayed amplified for a long time. I listened to sad songs and cried in my room for many, many, many hours.

The heartbreak was real, but the relationship left an impression on me of what love was supposed to feel like. Clint and I were friends first and then compatible in the most important ways. We made each other laugh. We believed the same things about God. Our puppy love felt equal and respectful. All these years later, I still count myself lucky to have had such a fun first boyfriend—until he got distracted by a redhead just before homecoming. But I don't hold a grudge or anything.

I measured every other person I dated against Clint Burns. Is it silly to compare a grown man to a middle schooler? Maybe. Is it ridiculous to build a just-past-puberty hometown boy into a legend he can't possibly live up to? Perhaps. But what that first love gave me was partnership, genuine care, and enjoyment. It showed me what it feels like to be in sync with someone. I loved and was loved a half dozen more times after Clint, but no one felt as close to home until I met Jeff, the man who would become my husband.

When I recognized in Jeff what had been present in my first, most innocent, and most equal love, I knew he was the one to cling to. It was above all else a compatibility, a synchronicity, between our bodies and our hearts. Would I have known this if I hadn't already experienced it as a young person? I don't know. Clint was there to teach me what love could feel like at the ripe old age of fourteen. I won't discount it just because we were young.

• • •

There are those friends who are there at the most critical moments. They show up. They hold your hand. They speak hard truths. They break through the fog and snap you out of it. This was my friend Shauna when she answered the phone on one of my darkest days.

When I met Shauna, we were both in our twenties and working at summer camp, the same one where I'd been a camper with Alli. I was a mere plebe counselor, and Shauna was in a leadership position, one of a few women among the men. She was one of my first examples of the type of woman I wanted to be. She wore her power loosely, but with total confidence. She didn't flirt to get her way; she didn't cast her eyes downward when speaking; she didn't apologize for her ideas. To the fifty or so young women on staff, Shauna was an example of womanhood most of us hadn't seen before. She spoke strongly, she walked strongly, and she laughed loudly.

We hit it off right away. We liked the same books and found the same things funny. Before we were even officially friends, people noted our similarities. Shauna and I spoke in the same patterns, used our hands and words in the same ways. We looked alike, too, or at least had similar styles and tastes. Even now, as women in our forties, we have been mistaken for sisters.

With two decades of friendship under our belts, most of which have involved me looking to her for advice and mentorship, one conversation in particular stands out. I still think about it all these years later.

It was summer, but neither of us worked at camp any longer. I was twenty-one years old, had graduated from college just weeks before, and was on the cusp of a move across the country, yet I'd been in a dark hole of depression since my boyfriend had unexpectedly dumped me and changed both of our futures. I was bereft. I could barely leave my bedroom. I only dragged myself into the shower when I was required to go to work, and sometimes not even then. I was lost and dirty.

Most of my friends were consumed with their own post-graduate lives or were unsurprised by the end of my doomed romance, so I couldn't talk about it much. One night, in a wave of self-pity, I called Shauna from the dusty, empty balcony of my temporary summer apartment. She answered the phone in Chicago, and I blurted out my confession.

"I gave him everything," I sobbed. "EVERYTHING," I emphasized, hoping she'd catch my meaning without me having to spell it out in humiliating detail.

I had given this boy everything and not by accident. Everyone within a hundred miles knew what would come next, but I had been blindsided.

Shauna listened to the broad strokes of my heartbreak and gave me a huge gift: she acted as if my poor choices were of the most ordinary kind. I didn't even know how much I needed to feel like my actions were normal. I was living in a bubble of hurt and shame, and she cared about what I was going through. Her acceptance was a relief. This was womankind. This was a club I was welcome in, with all its complications. Shauna ushered me right in.

"I can't get out of bed some days," I admitted. I readied myself for the optimism onslaught, for her to advise me to put one foot in front of the other, to put on my makeup as armor, to not let the man win. But instead she said, "Well, don't, then. Stay in bed."

My ears perked up. This was not what anyone else was saying to me. My parents didn't know what a mess I was in, and my coworkers had been politely averting their gazes, but I was imagining what I might say if I saw a friend who couldn't stop crying, who was on the verge of developing bed sores, and it wasn't, "Go back to sleep, sweetie."

Shauna also gave me a piece of wisdom way beyond her years, words I've clung to for decades now. She said, paraphrasing Anne Lamott, that when we are distracted by overwhelming emotions, when we are going through something messy and confusing and out of our hands, God is birthing something else in us that is just out of view.* That if we had our eyes on the new thing that was emerging, we'd inevitably get in our own way. We'd try to control it, or we'd mess it up before it really got going. So sometimes, when we are tangled up in some big, dramatic rollercoaster of a situation, the more important thing is making its way quietly into the universe. And when we're finally exhausted enough by our emotional entanglement and declare it over, we will look up and this new, better thing will be there waiting. We will have changed. We will have become something better.

Shauna heard me loud and clear, and she responded with exactly the thing my heart needed to hear, even though I didn't know it at the time. Her words helped me see that our mistakes or complicated circumstances aren't necessarily endings. They can be the start of something good and beautiful. She gave me permission to wallow in my breakup, to let it be as messy and awful as it was, and showed me that when I was ready, I could look for the promise of the new thing birthed. I trusted that Shauna knew what she was talking about, and the idea of this new thing on the horizon rang true.

---

* See Anne Lamott, *Traveling Mercies* (New York: Anchor Books), 107.

"Stay in bed as long as you need to," Shauna reiterated. "And then when you get up, it will be a truer getting up."

So I went back to bed. And I let the most important thing in my life be birthed while I was distracted by heartbreak. I was healing and evolving while I slept in a fog of sadness. Later that summer, I moved to California, and I stayed in bed for many days there, too. And then one day, months and months later, I awoke and stretched out my legs over the side of the bed. In a new place, with a chance to start fresh. And it was a truer getting up.

Shauna and I have stayed friends through life's unexpected twists, the kind of friends who can go years without seeing one another but then pick up right where we left off. She was there for me when it mattered, and in turn, I have become the friend who picks up a late-night phone call when someone needs me. I am forever indebted to Shauna for the thousands of words she's spoken and written that have left an imprint on my life, but it's that long-ago private conversation on the balcony of my college apartment that taught me how to be a better friend. She was there, offering so much grace and so little judgment. She made me feel normal and understood. She talked about God, not as a hammer or as a solution, but with the idea that I could make sense of my pain. All was not lost. I needed to hear exactly that, and her words have passed from my lips to my friends, and now to this page.

● ● ●

I knew Eddie Miller for about three months in 2001. Eddie was the older brother of a friend from college, and he had moved to Los Angeles a year or two before me, landing a job in post-production at a major studio.

Eddie's sister introduced us to one another via email before I moved to LA. He was the only loose connection I had in the city, and even though it made me nervous to rely on total strangers for advice on the biggest move I'd ever make, what choice did I have?

Over email, Eddie was funny and helpful. I was moving to LA with a friend I didn't know very well, and she brought job leads and apartment advice to the table through a family relation. I brought Eddie's big-brother familiarity to calm our nerves.

Eddie shared an apartment with three other people on the opposite side of town, and when he invited us over for the first time and introduced us to his neighbors across the hall, who had potted plants on their porch, I got *Friends* mixed with *Melrose Place* vibes right away. It gave me hope for the type of existence I could build in this scary new city.

For his part, Eddie seemed baffled by the arrival of two random girls on his doorstep. He was polite but wary. He took us to eat at a Thai place, and I was too scared to tell him that I only ate about four foods total, they were all white in color, and I couldn't even eat those if they were touching one another. My anxiety manifested itself in some prominent ways, not the least of which was through a limited variety of foods, but I worried that moving across the country without housing, or a job, or the ability to eat anything green would seem like a bad sign to him.

I suffered through the meal and hoped he wouldn't notice anything amiss.

I had lived in Los Angeles less than a month when planes struck the twin towers in New York City. My roommate and I didn't have a TV, and we got news of the terrorist attacks when a friend called before the second plane hit. We spent the next hour or so trying to get information through the dial-up internet connection to our old, clunky laptops, but eventually we called Eddie. Could we come over? Could we watch our country change on his couch?

A group of us sat in silence on Eddie's couch for most of September 11. The only small comfort came from being with other Oklahomans, other young people who were thousands of miles away from their families, who were equally worried that our new city was the next target.

I am embarrassed to admit that there was so much I didn't grasp about 9/11 right away. My mental fog (what I can now see as depression) didn't allow me to understand the gravity, even as I watched it with my own eyeballs. I was in shock, maybe, and disbelief. It took me a long time to cry. I observed the dull roar of LA mute itself to eerie silence on that Tuesday and the days that followed. We went to a patriotic singalong concert at the Hollywood Bowl just a few days after the attack, and I felt scared and numb watching the digital American flag wave on a JumboTron and fellow citizens wave their bodies along with the music. I was protected from the more graphic images and mounting hysteria by the lack of a television in our apartment, and after the first day, we just couldn't stomach going back to Eddie's couch ever again.

I came to understand 9/11 over the next months and years, not all at once, as it seemed everyone else did. I lost touch with Eddie before the end of 2001; we never seemed to make the hurdle past our initial shyness and then the shock of being together for the worst day in American history.

But he had hosted us, generously. He opened his home to two near-strangers at the most sensitive and confusing moment in the nation, and we all sat together in fear, an act of solidarity on his part. We were in it together that day.

●   ●   ●

I'm chatty when you get to know me, but I don't put out an approachable vibe. My face is generally not open. I don't want to chat with a stranger in a bar or with my seatmate on an airplane, almost ever. I'll make polite conversation if we end up in line together or something, but only if you initiate it and only if your opening line is interesting.

Paul and I were seated together on a direct flight from LA to Dallas. I was tagging along with my new husband, who was speaking on a panel at the Fort Worth Film Festival. Jeff and I boarded together, but we were booked several rows apart. I dropped my bag in the empty aisle seat, and an already-seated Paul looked up at Jeff and offered to trade seats with him.

Jeff, without missing a beat, winked, said, "No, thanks" and continued to shimmy sideways down the aisle. Paul looked startled. I laughed out loud, rolled my eyes at my husband, who believes a full plane is his personal sanctuary, and assured my seatmate that I wouldn't talk his ear off or anything.

We didn't stop talking until we landed.

Paul was an actor, part of a group who made comedies, and was also on his way to the film festival. We talked about all kinds of things, and before we touched down, he proclaimed that I would love his wife, Katie. We exchanged phone numbers for a future double date.

Those things don't usually take, right? You have a moment with someone in a circumstance in which you're stuck, and then later, when you look at the crumpled paper with someone's scribbled number or email, you feel silly. It feels weird to reach out. The connection seems lost, or you don't want to be the one to try to recreate it.

But we did end up getting together with Paul and Katie after the film festival weekend. And Paul was right: Katie and I hit it right off. I trusted her taste, her intellect, and her research implicitly.

We got together a handful of times over the next couple of years. Paul and Katie had a toddler son, then Katie and I discovered we were both pregnant with baby girls and due within just a few weeks of one another.

Katie was tall and elegant and carried her pregnancy more easily than I did. She took long, graceful strides while I waddled along and sweated through my tank top. But she became an invaluable resource for me. Overwhelmed by starting a family in Los Angeles, where the options are endless and the competition fierce, I opted to copy Katie's choices at every turn. She sent me to her OBGYN. And then later, when the babies were crawling, she suggested we join the local Mommy and Me music class, where her blonde-haired baby, Annabel, and my dark-haired baby, Lucy, would sit in a circle and put wooden musical instruments into their slobbery mouths.

I didn't know the first thing about trying to get kids into preschool in LA (did they even have preschool in Oklahoma when I was a kid?), and after a few fitful experiences, Jeff and I called Paul and Katie's preschool and applied for a coveted spot.

Not long afterward, Paul, Katie, and their two young children moved outside the city. And because life with little ones is busy, our friendship faded, taking the form of yearly holiday cards and occasional "likes" on each other's Facebook posts.

When Katie's name comes across my screen, though, I feel an immediate gratitude. Following her lead put me in the most capable hands when my first experience of childbirth went awry, and it put us on the educational path that finally brought the community I'd wished to have in LA for so long. I'm sure that if I hadn't met Paul on that airplane, I still would have found a doctor and a preschool for our kids. But it feels like they showed up out of nowhere at exactly the right time and just in time to point us down the right path. It was a short friendship that had long-lasting impact and led to numerous other relationships and choices that were good and right for our family.

We met Paul and Katie when we had no other local friends with kids. When we had no one else to ask our questions, they were there with all the answers. Here's what I learned from this: the answers are there, and they most often show up as people.

Your Turn

I want you to think about the people in your life who are hovering in your most important stories. They don't have to have major roles, although they might. Maybe they're ever-present like Alli at summer camp, or maybe they just happened to be standing there somewhat by accident, like Eddie, who provided the couch where we watched the worst day in American history and then never saw us again. This is a moment to acknowledge these people, either because they deserve it for showing up when it mattered—like my friend Shauna—or because they were a bit part in a story that deserves telling—like my first boyfriend, Clint.

If it helps, start by thinking of your most important days and then branch out:

Who came to your wedding?

Who showed up at the hospital with muffins for your
family?

Who was standing there when you got that phone call
(you know the one)?

Then make a list of the people who pop up in your various
memories:

Who was your childhood neighbor?

Who was the last person to help you out of a tight spot?

What former coworker brings a smile to your face after
all this time?

Do you have a significant life memory with a stranger?

And also, when have *you* been the one there, in someone
else's story? When were you a witness to someone's joy, or pain,
or that big event that never gets mentioned anymore?

Seriously next-level exercise: If it feels right (and you'll have
to do a gut check on this), reach out to one of the people you've
identified and say thank you, or tell them you'll remember
and never forget, or tell them how much they meant during an
important time. You can write a letter if you want to be really
formal, or write an email if that seems most appropriate. If
you want to ensure warmth is conveyed, call them on the tele-
phone, or better yet, say it in person.

You will rarely regret this type of expression of gratitude.

10 Things I've Learned from My Big Sister

There is something so beautiful about thinking of a loved one and writing down something about them. Making a list of the things you love about them, your favorite memories together, their quirks and quotations. By writing these things down, you're stamping them with love and gratitude. Bonus points if you're able to share the list with the one it's about.

My sister, Dawn, is nine years older than I am, which means that I was just eight years old when she left for college. In the years before that, we not only shared a room but shared a queen bed. I felt so safe sleeping next to her.

As sisters, we've always been close, even with the age gap. I was a freshman in college when her first child was born, my niece, Catherine Elizabeth, whose name is a combination of Dawn's and my middle names. By the time I had children of my own, Dawn had birthed three more kids and was a highly successful lawyer. She's taught me so much.

1. **The power of great nails and bold lipstick.** Yep, it was my sister who showed me how to assert yourself with these details, after she took a page from our mother's book. They both spent their careers wearing power suits and heels, whereas I spend most of my days in sweatpants. Still, we are women who are most comfortable with an intimidating shade on our lips.

2. **Christmas can be any day you want it to be.** When her kids were young, and my sister was juggling holiday commitments, she played fast and loose with December 25. Christmas Day arrived when she said it did. Can you imagine a bigger power move?

3. **Pray when it's hard (especially when it's hard).** Growing up, Dawn was the only person in my immediate family who shared my faith, and thus, she was the only person who talked about prayer. I watched her furtively at holidays when she was called upon to offer a word of gratitude, and then more openly as we aged and life got complicated. She has pointed me toward prayer, time and time again.

4. **It's better to be a big fish in a little pond. (Or is it better to be a little fish in a big pond?)** On and on, my sister and I have this debate. We disagree, we switch sides. We don't always land in the same spot, but I always come away from these types of conversations with a clearer understanding of what I value and why. It's invaluable to have someone to debate with who pushes you to clarify your position (and still loves you afterward).

5. **Believe the people you love.** Dawn believes every word out of my mouth. I'm not sure I can say that about any other person in my life. She believes my stories, and she believes my take on them. When my thought process evolves, she believes that, too. The older I get, the more I understand the value of someone who believes you, every time. I want to be this for others, but I'm not sure I could ever be as convincing as Dawn is when she listens to me ramble.

6. **Laugh loudly. It's okay if everyone hears you.** My sister has one of those bursting laughs, the type that makes people crane their necks in restaurants and movie theaters, looking for the culprit. We all make fun of her, but it really is such a joy. Laughter is contagious, and it makes things better.

7. **You can bear the unbearable.** Two of my sister's four children have endured significant medical issues that have left them fighting for their lives. These were unimaginable moments for our family, and Dawn handled these scary seasons with grace, wisdom, and strength. I hope I never, ever find myself standing helplessly by the

ice machine in the hospital ICU again, but if I do, I hope I'm once again holding hands with my sister.

8. **Nothing beats a shared history.** Being so far apart in age, Dawn and I joke that we grew up in different households. And in a way, it's true. Families and cultures change a lot in a decade, and being a child in the '70s looked pretty different from being a child in the '80s. Still, my siblings are the only people who understand my entire childhood. Our parents, our home, our pets, our stories—you can talk about these things in a different way with the people who were actually there. Being able to process all of these things with my sister has helped me so much during my mental health journey through therapy.

9. **Save yourself.** You know that old adage about putting on your own oxygen mask before helping others? In an incredible act of bravery, my sister chose to create a new life for herself and her four children all on her own, after spending years in a difficult marriage. This was hard, and it continued to be hard for a long time. Every day, I watched her walk through this difficult thing with courage because it was the right thing.

10. **Go first.** My big sister is the one who went first. I tried to emulate her at every turn. She went to prom, studied abroad, got a scholarship to college, got married, became a mother: all decisions I followed closely and some I flat-out copied to a tee. She went first. To this day, in the very middle of life, if we were standing at the mouth of a scary cave, I think she would take one look at her baby sister, face forward, and go first.

That's who she is.

What Are You Afraid Of?

We're all afraid of something. Some of us carry that fear more tangibly than others. I pull my hair out. You might cry or feel angry all the time. Maybe you want to feel fear as a means to feeling anything at all. Maybe you fear fear, and so you go out of your way to avoid feeling it. You stuff it down. You're vigilant about it.

Fear is powerful, which is why it is not easy to tell others about our fears. Talking about our fears makes us feel vulnerable, like we've strolled outside naked. Speaking our fears out loud can make us nervous that we might conjure the very things we're afraid of.

Like everything else, there are varying degrees of fears. We might be afraid of outside judgment. Snakes and spiders might make us woozy. I don't know a single mother who wouldn't name losing a child as one of her most prominent fears. To make matters worse, the internet stokes every scary thought we've ever had: the earth is burning; the government is spying on us; our bad habits are killing us. (All of these things are true, by the way. Which makes us more . . . wait for it . . . afraid.)

So why, then, this question? Why tempt fate and ask you to talk about your deepest fears? Because sharing our stuff drags it out of the dark and into the light, and everything looks better in the light. Maybe we'll see that what we're so scared of is just someone in a rubber mask. Maybe we'll see that we're all scared of the same thing. And that doesn't make it less scary, maybe, but at least the knowledge that we're not alone in our fears gives us a feeling of solidarity.

We're going to talk about what we're afraid of because when we give that big monster a name, we take away the beast's power and give it back to ourselves.

I'll Go First

I am afraid of snakes.

I am afraid of heights.

I am afraid of being betrayed.

But most of all, I am afraid I'm destined to be the victim of an in-home violent crime. And I don't want to brag or anything, but I had this fear long before the popularity explosion of true crime in pop culture made *everyone* afraid of being assaulted or murdered or robbed in their very own homes.

This fear of a lurking boogeyman is real, and it runs deep. It started when I was a kid, left home alone for hours at a time with a vivid imagination and a fondness for Stephen King novels. I discovered Stephen King when I was ten years old, thanks to the literary taste of a neighbor down the street who kept a row of horror paperbacks on a shelf out in the open. I pulled one down to thumb through it, looking for the scary parts (or the dirty words), and got so sucked into Mr. King's storytelling that I started bingeing on his work and never stopped. This episode followed an obsessive fascination with the sinking of the Titanic, so I guess I've always leaned toward the macabre. In addition to King, I read everything I could get my hands on that had a cover with its title in a cryptic font. R. L. Stine, Christopher Pike, and V.C. Andrews were staples when I was young. I liked ghosts and mysteries and anything with a sinister twist at the end. But the stories were just an outlet for a fear that was already there. The fear that something bad was destined to happen to me.

I was not the only person in my family who feared impending catastrophe. And the thing about growing up with a parent who thinks you're going to die at any moment is that then *you* think that you're going to die at any moment. My dad was always afraid for us. He looked for emergency exits in every room and insisted on sensible shoes for the airplane "in case we have to run." We always had a meetup plan in case someone got lost. Dad fretted endlessly about our safety.

(Two side stories from our family lore: When my brother was a teenager, he was crossing the street at the main intersection in our small town while my dad waited on the corner. An older woman ran the red light and hit Lance in the crosswalk. Mere moments after impact, he jumped to his feet to wave his hand and reassure Dad he was okay, then passed out cold in the street. Lance's first priority was to tell Dad he was alive. He was bruised and required some stitches, but he was fine. Dad still isn't over it. Another time, my sister Dawn was driving in a terrible rainstorm when her car hydroplaned and went into a deep ditch in the median. For years, my dad had preached at us that if we ever hit water in a vehicle, we should make sure to lower the automatic windows. We always laughed at this weird bit of advice. Why would we ever hit water? Who would think to roll down the windows if we did? But before my sister's floating car could sink, her hand hit the button to lower those automatic windows so that they opened before the power shorted out. This act likely saved her life. So are my dad's fears truly irrational or are they based in something supernatural? I'm still not sure.)

So, yeah, I grew up a little jumpy. And it is more than probable that my deep fear of catastrophe came from my generalized anxiety that something bad was going to happen to me combined with my steady diet of horror and thriller books. I thought I knew the difference between fact and fiction, but if you are what you immerse yourself in, then I was always waiting for the villain to appear.

And then something happened. Or rather, something *didn't* happen, but I'm convinced it almost did. I'm going to tell this story as plainly as possible, because it matters to me, and because it is the thing that turned a scared kid into a terrified adult.

I was twelve or thirteen years old, and our family was living in a rented house on the edge of town, nestled among trees and set back from a lone road that connected two highways. I was home alone after school, as usual, and stood outside barefoot in the warm sun, bouncing a ball against the garage door over and over in a soothing, repetitive motion. The afternoons were my time to decompress. While I bounced my ball, my lips moved silently. I made up stories in my head; I replayed conversations and gave them different endings; I spoke aloud my fantasies about being popular, or a famous gymnast, or a quirky genius writer. This was my self-soothing routine, and I was lost in my head when the van went by the first time. I must have clocked it, though, because when it creeped by again, I paid attention. I caught my ball and moved to the porch. The road in front of our house was paved but usually quiet. A car doubling back and passing again was almost unheard of. The van was white and rusted down the middle side panel. It looked exactly like every van adults had warned me about, like the one in every story that ended with a missing kid on a milk carton.

I got nervous enough to go inside, but I retained my wits until the van, on its third or fourth slow pass, made the slow turn into the driveway and idled toward the house. From my vantage point in the kitchen, where I was perched on the counter and peeking out the window, I could see the van's grill pointing straight at me. My heart started to hammer, and I slid down the wall until I was under the counter. My hand reached for the cordless phone and brought it to the floor with me.

This is it, I thought.

This is it.

This is it.

It's happening, the thing I've always been scared was going to happen.

I could hear the rumble of the old engine, now just a few yards away, where the van had come to a stop in front of the porch.

I could hardly think straight over the roaring in my ears. Had I locked the front door when I'd come in the house? I wasn't sure. I squeezed my eyes shut against all the possibilities playing in my mind. Was this really the end? Were all my fears of this very thing founded?

I called one parent and then the other, with no answer on either line. When I chanced another look out the window, the van remained in the driveway, ominous. I watched for some movement. The van was pulled too far forward for me to see the driver or if it held a passenger, and I couldn't see any activity near the front of the vehicle. Did that mean a person was just sitting there, or had someone gotten out and I'd missed it?

After a long few minutes that felt like weeks, I reached someone at my dad's law office, and I whispered frantically into the phone.

"I need help," I said. "I am very, very scared. There is a van."

To her credit, the woman on the other end of the phone acted swiftly. She put me on hold while she made a few phone calls of her own. Nothing changed while I waited, crouched and shaking on the kitchen floor, but it felt good to have shared my fear with someone on the receiving end. Someone who had the power to do something. Someone who, if these were my last words, got to hear them from me.

I was almost paralyzed by the fear of what might happen next, but I had to know if the van was still there and if someone had gotten out. I repositioned myself at an angle from below the counter so I could see just enough of the circle drive where the van sat idling, and concentrated hard on memorizing the exact shape and the rusty side panels so I could describe it later if necessary.

It was not my imagination that something was very wrong about the situation. I had been staying home alone after school for years. As nervous as I could be about unexpected occurrences, I had dealt with strangers ringing the doorbell, creepy phone calls, and the like. This was different. I knew it was different. I felt ice in my heart when I looked outside. There was evil there.

The woman from the law firm came back on the line to tell me she had tracked down a neighbor. This is a benefit of small town ways, where everyone knows someone who knows someone who lives close by. Before I could register that the van was starting to amble up and out of the driveway, I spied a man in boots and wranglers walking down the road to our house who fit the description I'd been given of the person coming to check on me. We were both startled when I threw my arms around him and sobbed, releasing my pent-up anguish from an episode that, if memory serves, lasted about twenty minutes total.

When my parents got home that night, they were confused by my hysterics. They were just sure there was some explanation. Maybe the van was checking out property, or maybe it was looking for the right address for a delivery. No, I said over and over and over again. No, no, no, no, no. I knew it was something bad. I could feel it. Something wasn't right.

My parents were sympathetic to my fear, but they didn't believe my gut instinct. They knew I read all those scary books in an effort to assuage my real-life fears of horror and assumed it was just my imagination run wild when surely there was an innocent explanation for why that old, crappy van had pulled into a driveway where a lone child had stood playing under the trees.

I stopped staying alone after that, for as long as we lived in that house. My hypothetical fears suddenly felt all too real. I started walking to the library after school instead, or went to friends' houses. It was fine if everyone thought I was being a little emotional over the whole thing; I'd just make the necessary adjustments myself.

● ● ●

My fear of something ominous happening to me did not abate with age. I moved from reading fictional stories about scary things to reading and watching true stories of murder or near-death experiences. I watched first-run episodes of *Forensic Files* and read book after book about famous serial killers and their crimes. It wasn't just entertainment for me; it felt like preparation.

When I left home, I went on to live in a college dorm, a sorority house, apartments with roommates, and then, eventually, alone. In all of these living situations, I could conjure fear of an intruder. Some of the groundwork was already laid for me: Ted Bundy had made sorority house murders into a common paranoia, so much so that one night, when I lived in the Theta house, we evacuated dozens of sleeping girls in the middle of the night because of a shifty man who wouldn't leave the parking lot. (This is a true story. And also, a few of our more upstanding members refused to decamp to boyfriends' living quarters, claiming they'd take their chances at being murdered before sleeping at a fraternity house.)

When I moved to Los Angeles, with a crime rate ten times that of anywhere I'd lived before, the stakes of being a young, single woman in the city got even higher. I did everything I could to feel safe, and most of the time, I did feel safe. One bonus of being part of an enormous population is that I always felt comforted that someone would hear me scream.

For most of my twenties, I never really got super scared, even while living alone. I stayed hyper-aware, but the particular fear of becoming the next *Dateline* victim took a hiatus for a while. My true crime consumption ramped up as it became more popular to portray tragedy as entertainment, but my real-life fears subsided.

And then I got a housesitting job.

Mr. Kody was the guest on a local news show where I was working for the day. He and his wife had just relocated to LA, and we struck up a conversation over the snack table. When I mentioned that the production gig wasn't my normal day job, and that I was just looking for ways to pad my bank account, Mrs. Kody asked for my contact information. A few days later, she emailed with an intriguing offer.

As it turned out, the Kodys traveled quite a bit and needed someone to care for their beloved cats. They didn't want me to simply feed and water the pets while they were gone; they said they would really prefer it if I would stay at the house for the duration. I could water the plants, bring in the mail, and see to other menial tasks. The pay was more than sufficient.

I leapt at the chance to earn easy money, but I was a little hesitant based on my quick assessment that the Kodys were high maintenance and particular about their home. Still, every dollar counted, and I had no real excuse to say no.

The Kodys' home high in the east Hollywood hills was breathtaking, with incredible views of the city. I was bowled over from the first time I set foot in the modern marble palace filled with art and sculptures and all-white furniture.

All things considered, their list of requests to me as a house sitter was pretty low. They had grown children, so the cats were now their great loves and took top priority. They were generous with their facilities, encouraging me to bring my laundry and—pointedly—boyfriends if I had them. I demurred the implied question.

They did have one condition: I must sleep in their master bedroom. At the time, this did not ring the alarm bells it should have. My brain was already churning over the idea of staying in this big, secluded house alone, and all my old fears were starting to crowd my mind while I attempted a polite smile amidst all the instructions. Also, the master bedroom was undoubtedly the prettiest, with floor-to-ceiling windows and a sprawling bathroom with not one but two huge glassed-in showers. In some ways, it felt like I was staying at a hotel for the long weekend. With cats.

I housesat for Mr. and Mrs. Kody every few months for years, and those days in that big, cold house were the only time I felt afraid during that season in my life. It wasn't just the quiet location or the insane square footage that made me feel unsafe. There was something else, something I could never quite put my finger on. Mrs. Kody was always appreciative and complimentary, and continued to insist I sleep in the master bedroom and that I was welcome to bring guests. I thought she was just being accommodating or trying to be "cool" to the young girl she paid to stay in her home. Until.

The Kodys had a few locked rooms in their home. I assumed this was for safety or that maybe there were very valuable things inside. I never thought anything about it until late one night, for reasons I don't remember, I turned the handle of a door to a room that had always been locked, and it opened. I found myself in a small space, probably meant to be an extra bedroom. The walls were lined with bookshelves, and there was a desk in the corner of the room with multiple computer screens configured on top. Beside the computer was unmistakably some advanced video editing equipment. And on the shelves, rows and rows and rows of tapes.

The tapes weren't labeled in a way that made sense to me, but I got chills with the sudden knowledge that there were cameras in the house. Cameras everywhere. And I must sleep in the master bedroom. And overnight guests were fine. And now I couldn't breathe.

I turned around, closed the door, and left the house immediately. I returned early the next day to feed the cats and retrieve my stuff, and then I vowed to never never never set foot in that space again. In light of the makeshift editing room in the home of a couple who had no business in professional production and had made no mention of a video editing hobby, a lot of the more unusual aspects of this housesitting situation started to make sense, and I felt sick to my stomach that I had let my desire for extra money eclipse my rational common sense and intuition. I'd talked myself out of listening to my gut instinct because the Kodys seemed relatively normal, and because it felt dramatic and dumb to believe them to be malicious. And yet here I was, in an obviously dicey situation. The weirdness of the Kodys reignited all my old fears of something sinister happening to me when I was unaware.

• • •

And then something did happen when I was very, very unaware.

On a beautiful September morning in the fall of 2018, I met an acquaintance at the door for a midday meeting. It was so beautiful outside that we decided to settle in the backyard, at the long outdoor patio table just steps from the house. The French doors to the kitchen and the upstairs balcony above us were thrown open, letting in the California sun and breeze.

Kelly and I worked outside for several hours, with laptops open and my dog, Kona Rocket, at our feet. I wandered in and out of the house to fetch water and then my wallet. My guest and I talked animatedly, making plans and dreaming big.

When it was time to walk Kelly to the door to leave, I led the way, chatting and talking with my hands. We entered the kitchen and walked toward the laundry room, headed through the house to where she had parked her car on the street.

I was so lost in whatever I was saying that I got almost to the door before I realized it had been broken in, shattered glass all over the floor.

I did not scream. Kelly couldn't even see why I had stopped so abruptly. I turned on my heel, and directed her to

Go back outside

Go back outside

Go back outside

Someone had broken into my house. Were they still inside?

I had my cell phone in my hand, and Kelly listened wide-eyed as I described calmly to 911 that there had been a home invasion, one possibly still in progress.

Despite all my years of fearing something just like this, the details were not what I expected. The day was so sunny. Everything was quiet, except that the birds were chirping. I was side by side with a person I barely knew. And we were trapped. The only outdoor gate was locked from the outside. When that realization dawned on me, my slightly delayed reaction sent my breath up into my throat.

With the phone still in my hand, I turned to face the house and stared hard at all the back doors open to the patio. Was that movement inside? Was someone about to come out after us?

Kelly and I stood paralyzed, not speaking, clutching arms. Relief washed over me when I heard the voice of the neighborhood security guy over the fence. He unlocked the back gate from the driveway, and as we hurried through, a sound erupted from inside the house, causing him to draw his weapon and Kelly and I to put our heads down as we fled. From across the street, we stopped and stood, breathless. In my driveway, the security man trained his gun on the back door, and we were all poised, ready to move at the next sound. It never came. We stayed in our positions until the police arrived and declared the house empty.

While we were waiting, pacing in disbelief, I went over the scenario in my mind. Kelly and I had been outside with the doors and windows open just feet from where we were working. We never heard the glass or door break. We never heard anything. My sweet dog hadn't so much as raised his head in alarm. I was busy tying the whole thing up in a bow in my head, deciding that maybe nothing had really happened. Maybe this was much ado about nothing, like the white van in my driveway all those years ago. Surely whoever had broken down the door had seen Kelly and me sitting outside chatting and had fled. We'd probably dodged a bullet.

This was my mindset when Jeff arrived from work after my shaky phone call full of apologies for bothering him over what was likely a near-miss. He waited with me outside while the police completed their sweep of our home and was standing beside me when the officer came out of the house looking grim.

"It's a mess in there," he said.

Jeff understood his meaning right away. I, on the other hand, was in such denial that I thought he was insulting the cleanliness of our home.

Our upstairs was ransacked. Our master bedroom and home office looked like a bomb had exploded. The intruder had dumped drawers, torn art off the walls, and pulled dressers and bookshelves out from their places. My beautiful jewelry was gone—every piece I'd ever received, including my wedding rings. Designer handbags and old electronics had also been taken. The rest of our stuff was just everywhere. On the floor. On the bed. Spilling out into the hall.

How could this have happened? How could someone be tearing apart your home while you sat in the yard, laughing and peaceful? This disruption had to have been loud, and it seemed impossible that we hadn't heard anything. Now that someone had actually broken into my home—and I had heard absolutely nothing—would this heighten my fear, even though I had not been harmed physically?

After the robbery, I stopped working from home for about a year. I joined a coworking space, and any time I was tempted to stay home alone and get some work done, the sun and the quiet and the birds chirping spooked me so badly that my hands would start shaking, and I would pack up and leave the house quickly. For a time, my fear of it happening again grew exponentially, and Jeff cut back on his travel. But after a few months of turning the robbery over and over in my mind, the acute fears did begin to dissipate. I didn't let go of the fear completely—I still feel nervous and superstitious now, as I'm writing this—but I somehow felt more in control of the outcome and less terrified of an unknown assailant.

My lifelong fear of becoming a victim to violence culminated in a home invasion that happened right under my nose, and with no resulting injury. It is my hope that it marked the end of these stories, these brushes of terror. I'm choosing to believe that for now, anyway.

Maybe our fears are based in the real possibility of losing the things most precious to us: a loved one, our health, our safety. Maybe they're an intuition of some kind working to protect our hearts, or maybe it's just culture preying on a primal human response. Or maybe we inherit the things that terrify us from generations that have gone before us and survived.

Fear, for the most part, seems to be about control. We are afraid of pain. We are afraid of uncertainty. We want to keep sad and scary and unhappy things from happening, even though we know it's futile. Pain comes. Hard things come. The only thing we can control is our response.

Your Turn

What are you afraid of?

I understand that the question itself is scary. Most of us have no desire to dig into our greatest fears. You may be thinking, *What's the point? This will only make me more afraid.*

But I want to reiterate that naming your fears takes their big monster power away. When you acknowledge that you fear something, the effort of pushing that thing down and away is removed, and you can feel how much energy you were giving to trying not to be afraid.

This might not translate to fears about roller coasters. Or spiders. But for the stuff that keeps us up at night? Trust me when I say that talking about it does not make it scarier. I wish I had investigated my fear of being murdered a long time ago. Would it have changed anything that happened (or didn't happen)? Maybe not. But I would have felt better. Sharing, in the right way and with the right person, always makes me feel better.

I respect your trepidation about answering *What Are You Afraid Of?* So let's talk about it.

Fears about sharing your fears:

1. **People will think you are being dumb.** Well, they might. The thing about fears is that they really run the gamut. My deep fear of snakes is irrational to my reptile-loving husband and children. They tease me about it endlessly. But if you're going to learn to be a sharer, you'll probably face the fear of sharing itself at some point. Once you've become a little more used to being vulnerable, you won't care so much if people think you're dumb. It's the paradox of sharing. Once you do it repeatedly, after you experience how it breaks the chains inside of you, you care a thousand percent less what others think about it. Truly.

2. **Somehow, by sharing your fear, you will manifest it.** I don't know if this superstition has any legs, but I get it. I don't like to say things out loud lest the universe take it as an invitation. But if you really think about it, do you truly believe that is how God works? Do you really think that a spiritual being misunderstands and takes a spoken fear as a wish and then forces it upon you? No. That just doesn't seem right. I don't believe that. It's too twisted.

   I do think we can learn great lessons from our fears. Whether they come up naturally—because many fears are part of life: heights, home invasions, disease, death—or you choose to confront them through therapy or role play or whatever—our fears can be our greatest teachers.

3. **You actually take comfort in your fears.** I know this doesn't apply to everything we're afraid of, but sometimes we might get so comfortable with our fears and

phobias that the idea of dropping them altogether is as scary as the fear itself. We can create cages around the things that scare us and then shape a life around them. I'm thinking of health obsessions, fears around flying, and sheltering our children to the extreme. If you think you might be taking a fear to a place that is regularly affecting your life or the lives of others, please seek some help. I want freedom for you.

Do you think you can tell someone about the things you're afraid of? Start with what scared you as a child instead of what scared you last week. And then, upon further exploration, see if those two things are related.

Symptoms of Anxiety (And 10 Ways I Treat Mine)

Let me be clear that I am not at all a medical professional. But I have spoken publicly about my lifelong struggle with anxiety and my journey to make peace with the ups and downs of mental health. I am forever indebted to those who have shared their own experiences with depression and anxiety, so I wanted to give you a basic idea of what anxiety feels like in my body and the tools I use to alleviate it.

What My Anxiety Looks Like

1. Can't take in a full, deep breath
2. Heart racing
3. Inability to yawn
4. Constipation
5. Headaches
6. Irrational anger
7. Weepiness
8. Looping, repetitive thoughts
9. Feeling impending doom
10. Unexplained body aches and pains

How I Feel Better

1. Mindfulness meditation

2. Hydration

3. Journaling

4. Deep, restorative sleep

5. Full-body massage

6. Doctor-approved medication

7. Pilates/yoga/dance/anything that engages the body

8. Therapy

9. Therapy

10. Therapy

Chapter

FOUR

What Were Your Pivotal Decisions?

I n chapter 1, we talked about the things that are decided for
us, and now we get to talk about the things that we decide. We
don't get to choose where and how and to whom we're born, but
we do get to decide how we'll play the hand we're dealt. These
are the choices that create or change our futures. Sometimes
they are active, ongoing decisions: to work hard, to break a toxic
family pattern, to move, to change, to believe in our own power.
And sometimes they are passive decisions: change coming at us
because we refused to make a decision at all. This is how the
universe works; it can be a real tangle to understand what is
our will and what is God's.

But there are a handful of times when our deliberate, con-
scious choices determine the path ahead. We remember these
significant choices, for better or worse. They are the major
milestones on our timeline. There was a fork in the road, and
we chose a direction. Our lives might have looked quite different
had we not made those pivotal decisions. It wasn't an accident.
It wasn't fate. It was a choice.

I'm sure some people have made pivotal decisions in childhood, but in this chapter, I want to focus on the decisions we've made as adults. For most of my life before the age of eighteenish, my choices were subject to factors out of my control and maturity. I have forgiven little girl Laura and teenage Laura for the choices that didn't serve their futures. And because so many of the decisions made for me were done in love and with excessive advantages, I deny those same versions of Laura full credit for the things handed to them. (To me.)

But once I hit twenty, from then on, my decisions were mostly my own. My race and education and socioeconomic status gave me an enormous umbrella of privilege; I will acknowledge that now and forever. No choice is without extenuating circumstances. But my parents were really, really hands-off. They taught me well and early that a person's life choices are their own. They told me this when I was six and whiny; they said it again when I was nineteen and sullen. "Choose wisely" was my first mantra.

When we start to make choices on our own, it's the ultimate trial and error. We may choose recklessly, see how that feels. We may try hard to be unobtrusive and invisible, so as not to burden anyone else with our choices. Like you, I've made decisions that have had longer-than-expected consequences, and I've looked backward enough to see when a series of small decisions affected my future.

But the big ones, the pivotal decisions? We each have only a few of those. Probably your most significant one has already come to mind.

What deliberate choices have you made that brought you to where you are today?

I'll Go First

For years I said, jokingly-but-not-really, that my first adult choice was breaking up with The Pastor. He was not, in fact, a pastor at the time. He was barely a man; we were practically still children. But he had a calling, and it was apparent to anyone who knew him for five seconds that it was a high one, a real one.

And I did not want to be a pastor's wife.

A pastor's wife, as he explained it to me, was its own sort of calling. One of submission and service. We would be a team, he said, working together, leading hearts into eternity. But as he pleaded his case, I think we both knew it was hopeless. When I made a casual joke about going panty-less in the front row of the congregation during his sermons, this normally hilarious man didn't find it at all funny.

The Pastor and I had known one another most of our lives, and in the beginning of our romantic relationship, we both believed our pairing was destiny. We were so well-matched in so many ways. If you put us alone together in a room, without the world in our ears, we had a blast. I thought he was the funniest person I'd ever met. Our eyes lit up at the sight of one another. We shared inside jokes that went back years.

But we didn't live in a vacuum. My changing beliefs and his calling mattered. He waited a long time for me to get clarity on my feelings, but when clarity came, it meant closure for our relationship.

I broke up with The Pastor in a ratty motel in Toad Suck, Arkansas, on the first day of the new millennium. The night before, he'd refused to kiss me when the clock struck midnight.

It was on principle, he said. New Year's Eve kisses were a construct of the culture he was counter to. I was superstitious about the meaning of a midnight kiss, especially as the clock ticked from 1999 to 2000, and my lips were barren at the end of the countdown. I took this final sign for what it was: an ending. A petty ending hidden in a huge decision.

I packed up my car and drove across the state line to my college town in Oklahoma. This was the only heartbreak I ever endured with my chin up, because I knew with absolute certainty I had made the right choice. Ending our relationship released us both from our bonds and propelled us into the better lives that awaited.

I called this decision my first adult choice because I didn't really want to break up with The Pastor. I loved him. I also believed he had a gift, and I could see that I didn't fit in the space beside him. I wanted to tease him from his pulpit for years to come. I thought our attraction might trump his theology. But I could see that this dynamic would eventually only leave us both frustrated and sad. We would have made one another miserable until the end of our days.

He might not agree with my version of events. I am leaving a very complicated story in the spaces between these paragraphs. (Pastor, I apologize if I didn't do you justice here. It's hard to write about such things. Let's agree, as you said in an email to me after my marriage, that we ended up with the right partners. The rest of it doesn't matter.)

I want to tell you something else about this story. Years and years after all of this, The Pastor came up in therapy. I gave my therapist the briefest overview of our love story, dismissing some crucial pieces of it with a literal wave of my hand. Again, with my chin up, I ended triumphantly with the part about it being my first adult decision. My therapist listened carefully, taking in my gesticulations, my spin. She stared back, and in her measured tone, she finally responded.

"Well, you really belittled his life."

"What?" I huffed. "No, I respected his calling. I truly believed he was meant to be a pastor, and I wanted him to go do that. I was *honorable* in this situation."

"You told him to go live out his calling with all but a pat on the head," she said. "You acted like you were too good for it. 'I won't be a pastor's wife.' Think of how he must have received that."

Tears sprang to my eyes. "No," I sputtered. "No. That's not what this story is."

She was right, of course, and I knew it the instant she said it. But I hadn't considered this take, not one single time. The narrative I chose to tell was magnanimous to us both. The Pastor and I lived happily ever after, separately. It was a good story told this way, but it wasn't wholly accurate. In my heart, I had questioned his calling—not whether he was capable, but why he would want that life in the first place. My big adult decision wasn't a letting-go-for-love the way I'd always told it. The truth was that my deepest held belief systems were already changing, but I wasn't ready to admit it then.

The stories we tell ourselves and others are not always the whole truth. Certain stories—like mine and The Pastor's—grow so ingrained in our psyches and in our personal narratives that we can't even see that they're not completely true, that they're not objective.

In order to follow our best paths, maybe we don't need to consider every angle of every single possible outcome, nor do we always have to consider the desires of everyone around us.

Trying to make pivotal decisions that way would be exhausting, impossible, and paralyzing. When I left The Pastor behind in Toad Suck, I was twenty and in the exact time of life when it would be a mistake to get tangled up in the expectations of others. It was the right decision, and I'm glad I made it. But it was not exactly cut and dry.

Thinking about your own life as you read this book, make room for the possibility that some of the things you believe to be absolutely true are actually just stories. Some part of them made you who you are. You created the narrative based on the information you had, or on what your heart could handle, or on what the world forced on you. But someone else might see things differently. Not the facts, but the feelings. We can hold all of this in our hearts at the same time.

● ● ●

My decision to move to Los Angeles didn't come in a single moment, but once it was made, it felt like the most natural next thing. I came back to college in Oklahoma after studying abroad in England and knew I needed to change up my surroundings. I couldn't shake the nagging feeling I'd ignored my whole life that I didn't fit in a small town. I wanted to be somewhere big, where I could succeed or fail in private. I wanted to disappear into a city with a huge population, where no one had any expectations of me. With the world at my feet, freedom felt like starting somewhere new, reinventing myself in the middle of the action.

When you grow up in the middle of the United States, there are really only two places to go and feel like you've made a big leap: New York City or Los Angeles. Opposite coasts, opposite cities in many ways, both looked upon as highly suspicious and sinful by those in God's country. I was too chicken to go to New York City. This country girl feared the subway, feared people on top of people, feared fifth floor walk-ups and dirty snow and having to learn a new way of life. With nothing to lose and no real plan, I decided I didn't want to be cold. California called to me, and LA seemed like the only place in America that would scratch my particular itch to become someone new and glamorous in a place far away.

I didn't know then that moving to Los Angeles seeking fame and fortune when you're young is a cliché, but it likely wouldn't have deterred me if I had known it. The people who pilgrimage to LA and end up here confused and battered are among the most interesting I've ever known. But you can't know that before you join their ranks. It's impossible to explain until you've done it yourself. The thing is, you can be anyone you want in LA. You can try on a new identity every week if you want to. No one had spelled that out for me when I was still dreaming about palm trees and movie stars, but subconsciously, I was drawn to a land of seekers and free spirits.

In a pattern that would repeat itself throughout my life, I started verbalizing my dream to everyone around me in the hope that saying something out loud over and over would make it so. As friends started interviewing for jobs or applying to graduate school, my senior year refrain became, "I'm moving to LA." That was it. No plan. No job. It was the movement that mattered. The rest I would figure out on the fly. I'd never even been to Los Angeles. But I was so singularly focused on the destination, I didn't care about the process of getting there, and I had no inkling what would happen after I arrived. Some pivotal decisions are just like that. You know they're right, even when they don't make any sense.

My boyfriend at the time, Sebastian, agreed to move to Los Angeles with me for his own reasons that had nothing to do with mine. He liked skateboarding and music and West Coast culture, and maybe he liked that I was determined enough to make such a pipe dream happen. I don't know. I can't speculate on it too much. Our relationship took up so much of my heart for so long that I can no longer discern what is truth and what is mythology. It doesn't matter much to the story anymore, anyhow.

What matters—what is important about how it all unfolded—is that during the few days between my college graduation and a scheduled trip to LA to look for a place to live, Sebastian walked into my empty apartment and unceremoniously dumped me. My hair was wet and wrapped up in a towel. He was wearing a motorcycle jacket that he left on for the few minutes it took to break up with me. One day we were planning the next stage of our life in California, and the next day he ended our relationship so severely that it was as if he had died right there in that small, carpeted bedroom.

He wasn't the one who died in that moment, but a part of me did. I'd spent the better part of a year planning my great escape from my home state, with my eyes on the prize of a big adventure. We hadn't left yet, but I could feel myself already starting to grow and expand into the person I wanted to be, the version of myself who made a life in LA. Making those plans with Sebastian had given me courage. Now I was doing it alone.

During the next few weeks, my heart apparently kept beating; my eyes opened and closed. But Zombie Laura had taken over, and it was Zombie Laura who, curled into a fetal position on the airplane flying over Orange County, decided that nothing would derail her move to Los Angeles.

I'd made the decision to move to the West Coast almost exactly a year prior, swearing that, come hell or high water, I was going to do this next right thing. How could I have known that there would be both hell and high water?

Ultimately, it didn't matter if the move to Los Angeles came as a result of having talked about it for so long or if I moved forward with my plans out of resentment for the person who had made me a lot of promises and then broken them; it didn't matter if Zombie Laura was doing the heavy lifting, putting one foot in front of another while the rest of me took a long, deep, heartbroken nap.

What mattered is that I followed through on my decision. I didn't doubt in the darkness what I had known in the light. I had said I was going to do something, and I did it. I did it with the safety net of family behind me and with the false bravado of a young person, but who cares? If I had decided to move back to Oklahoma within the year, I still could have claimed victory. I had made a decision and stepped forward in faith. It was the choice on which the rest of my life hinged. Moving to Los Angeles—even as the hot mess I was at the time—bore out all of my life's greatest dreams. I was able to dig deep and find myself and who I wanted to be, away from the trappings of a conservative culture that wanted to make me smaller, quieter, and more compliant. I thrived in LA almost from minute one, and I've never looked back. More than any other single decision in my entire life, moving to California was the most pivotal.

I sometimes wonder if these huge decisions are also the easiest ones to make. Oh sure, we'll hem and haw and make pro and con lists and seek counsel from sources to either con- firm or deny what we've already, deeply and secretly, decided.

But when people tell me about their pivotal decisions, it seems like the biggest ones come as naturally as water flowing. Choosing a partner, a job, a school, a location. Leaving a marriage, a career, a country. There is an undeniable pull to choose what is right. We don't always heed that pull, of course, and then what follows is resistance down a bumpy road. But when we turn away from a thousand wrong decisions and toward one right one, the energy flows differently. There is an ease to our words and our spirits.

Moving to California from Oklahoma was not a cakewalk. The culture shock started when my brother arrived in his pickup truck, pulling a flatbed trailer loaded with everything I owned down Hollywood Boulevard, and it didn't end for a long time. I looked and sounded like a hillbilly in a world of beautiful bodies and untraceable accents, but I didn't care. Los Angeles welcomed me like it did all the other throngs of starry-eyed dreamers, which is to say without notice and with the expectation that I'd assimilate.

And it was easy to stay in Los Angeles. The first year went by in a blur, and then it had been two years, and then six. Every time I went back to Oklahoma, it solidified the fact that I didn't want to live anywhere besides Southern California, at least not that year and not the year after.

I chose to stay even when other opportunities arose. I chose to stay when I was the only person I knew who voted for George W. Bush. I chose to stay even when nieces and nephews were being birthed back in Oklahoma at a rapid pace. I missed every important family event, and the unimportant ones as well.

The longer I stayed in California, the more I became a Californian. Eventually, I dropped any fantasy of living in any other part of America. It happened slowly and quietly, but after fifteen years, the transformation was complete. I woke up and decided never to live anywhere else.

• • •

I am self-conscious that two of my three stories about life's pivotal decisions revolve around romantic relationships. If I could make this fact be somehow less true, I would. But I'm committed to being honest in these pages, and thus, I have to admit that the best pivotal decision of my life was convincing Jeff to marry me.

When Jeff and I met, I was a twenty-two-year-old production assistant. He was thirty-five and on his second successful career. We worked together for over a year before we started carpooling from our shared neighborhood in Hollywood to the MTV production offices in Santa Monica. That commute is roughly an hour each way, so we were spending two hours alone together in the car every weekday. Mostly I drove, and he paid for gas and breakfast. This was before smartphones, so distractions were at a minimum. We listened to music; we rode in companionable silence. We also talked a lot, about all kinds of things.

Jeff was my boss, so there were physical and emotional boundaries in place from the get-go to which we strictly adhered. Still, it was a lot of time in the car. Months on end of being stuck in traffic together for ten-plus hours a week will cause a bond to form between you. We could each read a mood in the other without a single word. We memorized each other's drive-thru food orders and what songs on the radio could change the vibe quickly. We ceded control to one another's driving habits in traffic.

We talked a lot about work and the TV show we were making. He had to listen to me talk about friends back in

73

Oklahoma. We shared our pasts, both the glowing parts and some of the ugly stuff.

Jeff and I stayed squarely in the friend zone for years before anything romantic happened between us. We didn't so much as hug hello or goodbye. But he was the first person I saw each morning and the last person I saw before heading home for the evening. Our days were organically built around our time together, and slowly, that commute time started to bleed into our free time. We'd grab dinner in order to miss traffic. We'd run errands together on the weekends. On New Year's Eve 2004, a festive hug lingered a little too long . . . but that was it.

We were working on the show *Wildboyz*, a spinoff of Jeff's hit TV show, *jackass*. In the early spring of 2004, the crew was on a month-long shoot to India and Indonesia, a production trip that wasn't going smoothly. It had been a series of long, stressful days, and Jeff would regularly find excuses to call me back in LA where I was stationed at the production office.

I had taken advantage of this forced separation to reset a few things in my personal life. I knew by then that I was in love with my boss, and I was fairly sure my feelings weren't reciprocated. I was starting to feel like an idiot. While Jeff was away in Asia, I took up a friend on the offer of a blind date setup. It felt good to move in a positive direction and not a dead-end one. It felt good to be out with someone who was plainly interested. There were no work boundaries, no age gap, no games. We went out a few times, and then Jeff came home.

He sounded exhausted when he called from his house up the hill from my apartment.

"When it got hairy," he said, "all the guys were calling home to their wives or girlfriends or moms."

I waited.

"I just wanted to call you," he finally muttered.

We met at our favorite bar, somewhere we usually went with a large group of rowdy friends. This time we were alone, wedged together in the red leather booth and yelling over the music. Jeff ordered shots, even though I didn't drink shots. We needed the quick confidence. We had known one another for over two years, and this was the moment of reckoning.

The problem, as Jeff saw it, was that it would be impossible to dabble in a romantic relationship with me. He was my boss. We were in the same social circle. It was going to get complicated quickly, and if we became a couple, there would be no going back. I was also clear from the beginning that I wanted a family and was intent on the idea of being together forever. As someone who had proclaimed long and loud that he never wanted to get married and never wanted children, this pained him. But I saw through that bit of bravado. Our liquid courage at the bar led to a first kiss, which led to the official beginning of our most important love story. But it wasn't without bumps in the road. Our decision to transition a friendship into a romance cost us our working relationship and created some discomfort in our wider group of friends.

It took us awhile to work out the kinks. And then, after two years of dating, we found ourselves at yet another crossroads when I was ready for a more permanent commitment and Jeff wasn't. By then, I was twenty-seven and he was forty, and I was singularly focused on the future while he was content to let things stay the way they were. It took some convincing on my part to make this man marry me. Although I can joke about it now, and everything worked out beautifully (just like I knew it would), I wouldn't recommend this particular relationship dynamic before marriage. I would be appalled if my daughter felt she had to persuade someone into such an important decision. It's tricky, though, two people falling in love and being ready for the next stage at the exact same time. It took a lot of long talks, a few tears, and working to create a shared vision of the life we wanted together. Realistically, I think Jeff and I were mostly just lucky. Our relationship was built on mutual respect, and choosing the other in marriage required real trust on both sides. By the time he proposed, we were in sync on this monumental decision and in such a peaceful place. We exchanged vows on a gorgeous fall day in front of everyone we loved.

Over the years, I've spun our love story various ways, from pretending I clubbed Jeff over the head and dragged him down the aisle to acting like I am the rightful wife who took her place beside her man. But the fact remains that I was the driving force behind our marriage, and I don't regret it. I knew he was the best person I'd ever met. I knew he would make an excellent husband and father. I knew, after thousands of hours battling the LA freeways together, that we made a good team. Choosing a partner and a co-parent is one of the biggest decisions a person ever makes. For this one, I deserve a gold medal.

Your Turn

Not all of our most momentous decisions are made in total independence. Sometimes important decisions are made in collaboration, or out of desperation. Think about your biggest decisions, the circumstances around them, and why you did what you did. Do you feel lucky in how the results shook out?

Or would you do it differently if you could? Maybe a combination of both?

I highlighted a few of my biggest life decisions (a breakup, a move, and a marriage) but yours will likely look different. A few examples of decisions that may have changed your path:

What type of education did you choose (or not choose)?
How did you decide where to live?
What job or position has had the most impact on
    your career?
Why did you want to marry that person?
Has a friend ever been part of a big decision?
What act of kindness made an impression on you?
Have you ever made a reckless decision that affected
    your future?
Have you ever made a big decision that involved buying
    or selling something?
When has the decision to "unfollow" served you well?
Have you ever offered or received an apology that saved
    a relationship?
When have you made a decision to share yourself
    vulnerably?

Consider the stories you've told about your own pivotal decisions for so long that they've become myth. Would someone else tell them differently? Is there a chance you've made yourself the hero in a decision that was actually inevitable?

Our decisions become the plot points of our lives. We can look at the past as a straight set of facts, or we can notice the small choices that led to the most pivotal moments as insights into the narrative of our lives.

Pieces of Unsolicited Advice

In my real-life friend group, I am known for being bossy. I do not mind this label. If I could give you 10 pieces of totally unsolicited advice for life, it would be these things:

1. **READ.** Reading broadens the mind, heart, and spirit more than anything else on earth. The next best thing for broadening one's worldview is travel. Not everyone can travel, but everyone can read.

2. **Set a timer.** I set timers for everything (including reading). You can get a lot more accomplished in twenty minutes than you think, so set the timer and knock out a task, fit in some type of pleasure you've not made time for, or make small progress on a big project. I live my whole life by timers.

3. **Learn to listen to your intuition.** Intuition is your best life tool, but it can easily get muffled by the noise of the world. Try sitting for just five minutes a day in total silence, having asked yourself a question and listening for the answer. If your brain is too noisy, try freewriting your answer until something emerges that feels right in the deepest place. Train yourself to tune in.

4. **Dress for the day you want to have.** My friend Abby coined this phrase, and it works. Clothe your body and adorn your face and hair as the person you want to be. Dress for success, or for a good time, or for peaceful relaxation, or as a polished, confident human. When you feel like you look good, you will act like you look good, and something will emanate from within.

5. **Prioritize your physical space.** More and more and more I have come to believe this. Whether you live in a shared studio apartment

or a mansion on a hill, make every effort to create a space that fosters what you value: creativity, coziness, peace. Surround yourself with objects that bring you joy, colors that make you feel a certain way, and light that motivates or soothes. This is not about stuff; this is about energy.

6. **Don't be late.** A few years ago, I hosted an online habits challenge wherein participants attempted to make or break one habit each month. One of the challenges centered around being on time everywhere you go. When I was forced to get super mindful about my timing, I was shocked at the difference it made in my day. I realized I was living with near-constant, low-grade anxiety by rushing: stressing out because I was already late, getting annoyed by traffic, panicking when I couldn't find a parking spot. Being on time everywhere every day alleviated about fifteen levels of unnecessary stress I didn't even know I was holding onto.

7. **Take the selfie.** You are beautiful. You ARE. Also, years from now, in the future, you will never regret having photos of yourself, and it won't matter that you're the one who took them. Stop the selfie shame.

8. **Pay attention to what you skip.** I want you to start noticing what you skip, what you scroll quickly past, and what you purposefully ignore. Your friend who posts articles about social justice issues that make you uncomfortable? The cousin who details her weight loss journey? That sad movie everyone keeps talking about? If you consistently get a twinge inside around certain topics or people, you should investigate why. That may be a pain point that needs attention.

9. **Forge a mind/body connection.** Our bodies are always speaking to us, and they are telling us the truth. Learn to interpret pain, aches, headaches, digestion trouble, or anything else that may be a warning sign about your emotional state or physical environment.

Especially as we age, the tension between mind, body, and spirit can become fraught and often even disconnected altogether. Neglecting either your body or your spirit will eventually affect its counterpart. Attempt to have them work in tandem.

10. **Teach people how to treat you.** I think this is a Dr. Phil quote, but I originally heard it on *Oprah*, and it has become one of my most important life mantras. This truth applies to everyone around you. If someone is unkind to you, and you stay silent, you have inadvertently taught them that it's okay to direct meanness your way. On the other hand, if you require respect, you are more likely to receive respect. I haven't nailed this one, but I keep it in mind all the time, and try to apply it across the spectrum of relationships. From children to business partners, you teach people how to be in relationship with you.

Chapter FIVE

Who Taught You How to Be?

A s much as we would all like to believe we are true originals—like all the songs say and like our mamas told us—we're really a collage of the people around us and those we imitate. How we quilt it all together is what becomes unique about us, but from the time we emerge, warm from the womb, someone else is teaching us how to be.

We learn first from our families. The love our parents bestow or withhold becomes one of our first messages about where we fit in this world. Our siblings, if we have any, are some of our most important early influences. Through them, we learn to mirror and negotiate. In our families of origin, we are taught the rules of the world. Every day we are given rapid-fire instructions of how to be: quiet, loud, joyful, angry, polite, rebellious. And we also take in unspoken family rules: be silent, stand up for yourself, smile, don't anger Mommy, always look pretty, work hard, don't inconvenience others, show your love, make good choices.

When we get a little older, it's our peers who show us how to be socially acceptable by reinforcing the way we act or by shaming it out of us. We don't understand when we're young *that everyone else is also learning how to be in the world from their families of origin, and we are impressed by those who seem to know how to be in the world better than we do. And so we try their actions on for size. We get a little sassy because we saw Susie get sassy, and that seemed empowering. We ask for a certain brand of shoe for Christmas because our friend looks so cool when she wears them. And looking cool feels important for many, many, many years, until we snap out of that fantasy. (Hopefully we do snap out of that fantasy.)*

Around the time we realize our peers don't have it any more figured out than we do, outside forces start to worm their way into our psyches. We try to imitate characters we see on TV or in the movies as well as older kids and adults we aspire to emulate. During my lifetime, I've tried to change the way I walk, the way I dress, my accent, even my social media feeds based on what someone else was doing. I like the way that person is showing up; I want to show up that way, too.

It's natural for us to try on different ways of being in the world. Many of those behaviors and attitudes fall away, but some stick because we realize they reflect our true selves. And that can feel good and right.

Even the strongest personalities take on the traits of others, consciously or subconsciously. To a large extent, I believe in the old adage that we're all an amalgam of the five people we spend the most time with. Looking back at different seasons of my life, when I think about who those five people were at any given time, I either want to cringe or crow. It's so true. Someone is always teaching us how to be.

I hope you were surrounded with love from the moment you were born. When you look back at those who influenced you the most—from immediate family members to fictional characters

to your best friends to cultural leaders—I hope you feel lovely
gratitude for the people who taught you how to be. And if you
can pinpoint those people who did not bring out your best self,
well, I hope it brings about an aha moment.

I'll Go First

I was the third and final baby in my family, wanted and loved,
but not without complication. My mom developed toxemia
late in her pregnancy with me, putting us both at risk. And
although the family plan had been to have another companion
baby after me, my mother's health and my father's fear put
an end to that idea and left me dangling at the bottom of our
family, seven and nine years younger than my two siblings,
respectively. So I was born into a world with an abundance of
people to teach me how to be, and I showed up eager to learn.

The primary values in my family were intelligence, attrac-
tiveness, and self-efficiency, and all of those things needed to
be effortless. If you were trying hard at something but it didn't
come naturally, then it was not meant for you or for the family.
My siblings and I were assumed to be smart; we were given
all the tools to make ourselves attractive, and we were taught
early that being self-reliant and never an inconvenience to
others would reap life's highest rewards. I took in all of these
messages and acted accordingly.

Luckily, I was an easy baby and grew to be compliant and
bookish, preferring my own company to outside activities.
When I was nine, I started staying home alone after school.
I made decent grades, and by high school had taken religious
vows not to drink or have sex. I fell in line with every family
rule, including the unspoken one about not drawing any undue

attention to yourself, good or bad, at any time. I stuffed down my crippling anxiety and suffered my fears in silence so as not to cause anyone concern.

But starting early, my eyes were often scanning the room for other ways to be. There was something big within me I didn't have an outlet for and wouldn't dare release. It felt like an orb that lived in my center, between my stomach and my chest—like one of those electric balls from the science store where all the crackling current goes when you touch it lightly. There was a buildup of energy inside me that didn't go with my exterior.

So when I was introduced to various fictional characters of outlandish femininity who were in charge of their homes and lives, characters with sharp wit, dramatic outfits, and a brazen boldness to how they walked in the world, my soul sang out.

It was my dad who introduced me to Auntie Mame via the classic film, based on the book by the same name. Auntie Mame, played by Rosalind Russell, is a wealthy, opinionated, independent woman whose life is rocked when her nephew, Patrick, is suddenly orphaned and dispatched to live with her. Dad was light-heartedly into Hollywood, and he presented Auntie Mame's character as if she was a real hoot. Contrary, I'm sure, to how he would feel if he knew anyone in real life who resembled Mame Dennis. In rural Oklahoma, we knew no one like Mame Dennis, with her sequined mumus, exotic cocktails, and modern New York City apartment.

But until I met Auntie Mame, I had no idea this was even a way to BE in the world. Mame Dennis was ridiculous, but she was also funny and respected in her own way. She had parties and lovers and, most importantly, she did the right thing when it mattered: she took in her nephew when he needed her, without complaint or outsourcing. I watched the screen in awe as she swept down the staircase with a flourish, wrist bangles dangling, the star of every scene simply because of the way she moved and glittered. Mame loses her wealth, another husband, and for a time, even her relationship with an adult Patrick, but she does so with dignity and humor and every bold accessory she can fit on her body.

I was a bit older when the movie *Troop Beverly Hills* debuted. The movie begins with Phyllis Nefler, played by Shelley Long, facing a scandalous divorce and, with it, the loss of her money and status. Her middle-school-aged daughter (played by Jenny Lewis, who was just about my age when I first saw this movie) is the most stable member of the family, more mature by far than her mother. Phyllis—who wears outrageous clothes and hairstyles, is high-maintenance in every way and comically obtuse about it—finds a way to support herself, connect with her daughter, and slay the bullies, all while keeping her trademark style and humor intact.

Look, I realize these movies are not exactly timeless, and they both have problematic themes. The fictional women who shined a light on my future path are actually caricatures of the privileged, high-maintenance wealthy woman, and the audience is meant to find them slightly despicable, I think, in spite of their beauty and charm. But I didn't understand those elements back then, at least not fully. What I saw in Auntie Mame and Phyllis Nefler was strength when everyone else thought they were dumb. I saw style where others saw tacky. I saw love outweighing selfishness. I saw women who persisted, even when society tried to write them off.

And I wanted to be like that. I *was* like that, I felt, inside. When I met those women on the screen, I was a plain child who hid behind her tangled hair, read books, and bounced a ball alone all day; a girl who pulled out her hair and stuffed down her pervasive fears in order to muddle through social situations. But now I had a beacon pointing me toward who I wanted to be when I grew up. I was going to help people. I was going to do it wearing lipstick.

Roughly two decades later, I named my blog *Hollywood Housewife*. Whenever there was confusion over this branding and whether it was meant to be mocking or taken seriously, I always felt like it was both of those things, a not-so-subtle throwback to Mame and Phyllis.

The only real-life example that even came close to the feminine force of these fictional women were our small town's society ladies. My own mother was a working woman, wearing power suits and sensible heels every day. She had a corner office and took no nonsense. My mom liked pretty clothes but didn't want to stand out. Her strengths led in a different direction. She favored facts and numbers and mistrusted drama and whimsy. She was not friends with the women who lunched and did not understand my fascination with them.

On the whole, the society ladies were congregating in places where I was not. So I didn't get to see up close what this particular type of housewife was like until I was old enough to understand what I was observing. These were not Stepford wives. They were the opposite of that cliché, really. Their observations were sharp as knives, and they were often playing an intellectual chess game that was levels above their husbands'. They dressed well and took care with their faces, and they were up-to-date on art, fashion, and cultural references that extended well beyond the scope of our county lines. I was enamored.

What I saw in these women was a subversive power and not an overt one. Men were still the elected officials, the leaders, the business owners. But their wives were quietly running a different sort of show, and, from my seat in the audience, a far more interesting one. They were a quick study in outwardly professing one thing—that, as wives, they played a secondary role to their heads of household, for example, if the conversation turned to that—and letting every action speak for itself, showing who was really in charge.

The society women taught me a lesson in How to Be in an area of the country that still considered feminism to be the worse f-word.

I always assumed my life would look like theirs someday, so I modeled myself after these women for a time. I planned to marry a nice man and have a clothing budget, and believed I would sweetly seize whatever power was there for the taking. It didn't seem like a bad life.

It hadn't occurred to me yet that I might leave Oklahoma, so in the interest of staying put and serving the hand I was dealt, I started shopping at the same stores where the society ladies took their daughters, I joined the clubs that led to sororities that led to more clubs, and I pulled pages out of magazines as I planned for a future dream home.

I thought, quite incorrectly, that these women were mini Mames, more reasonable Phyllises. But I understand now that they were real people. They weren't characters, and they certainly weren't caricatures, and the strength they were forced to display over the years as they grappled with bad marriages, loss, wayward children, and a secular cultural revolution was real and unaffected by their pearls and brushed silk jodhpurs. They showed a strength and wielded a power I still don't fully comprehend because I left Oklahoma before I was done figuring it out.

After I'd been in Los Angeles for more than a decade, after I was my own sort of housewife, even taking on the public moniker that was inspired by them, I had a series of encounters with these women, together and individually. Time had marched on, it seemed. I hadn't grown up to be them. We both seemed glad for that.

* * *

I met Sam on the first day of sorority rush week during my sophomore year of college. Her reputation preceded her, however, as she was known then and forever as the freshman Theta who had egged the Pi Phi house, nearly getting her kicked out of Greek life. I couldn't imagine what on God's green earth would compel someone to drunkenly throw raw eggs at such a stately mansion. Nor did it make sense that Sam would become one of the most important figures of my college years.

For our first official rush week as members of Kappa Alpha Theta, tasked with recruiting potential new members, we were sorted into random groups to study the incoming rushees and to learn our various house songs and procedures. I'd spent most of my freshman year overwhelmed by my 200-plus sorority sisters, each of whom seemed more beautiful and poised than the last. I was out of my depth and spent a good deal of time just keeping my head down. In our cordoned-off rush group, though, Sam stood apart from the other ponytails of perfection. She was highly irreverent about the process and made me laugh out loud at her shrewd observations and self-deprecating humor. She could contribute meaningful analysis while in the same breath she made fun of the lengths we took to convince gaggles of eighteen-year-olds that we were the best sorority on campus.

Sam was an entertainer, and I was more than willing to be entertained. She recognized quickly that the nerdy girl in the corner caught her jokes and laughed every time. To my immense surprise, our cautious judgment of each other blossomed into a lasting, opposites-attract friendship. She was a leader; I was a follower. She was the star; I was the audience. She was the rebel; I was the good girl. We were an unexpected balance. Being friends with Sam loosened me up. She taught me how to relax. She taught me how to be fun.

In college, I was a little slow to find my footing. Being a part of the sorority was playing out my deepest belonging dreams, and it was a first for me to become friends with some-one who didn't need all of that in order to feel like she was exactly where she was supposed to be. The youngest of five and with four older brothers, Sam knew how to take a punch and how to give one, with her fists *and* with her words. She was a blonde-haired, blue-eyed powerhouse, and most of our pledge class was intimidated by her. I loved being friends with her.

When Sam took me under her wing, it felt like I had both protection and defense. She didn't let her party-hard friends tease me, and she didn't let my Pollyanna friends keep me from her. She said we were a team, and I took that as gospel. We had a third best friend, Jenny, and our trio felt complete. Together, they taught me over and over again not to take things so seriously, to laugh, to let myself be a little crazy. Intimidated and balancing an anxiety disorder, I was fortified by a friendship with such confident, leading women.

Early on, Sam showed me that there was more to me than

what I projected on the outside. I was starting to grow up emotionally, and for the first time, I had influences outside of my small town and small family and small church. College was doing what everyone had warned it would: it was expanding my mind. Sam was a close witness to that expansion. When the cracks in my cultural experience showed—and they showed often—she was paying attention. I was such a pleaser. I minded authority; I followed the rules. I held my religion and my every relationship tightly. Sam filled in the blanks, answering all my questions without making me feel stupid for not knowing anything about sex or drinking or about the girls who were lying about sex and drinking.

"What's special about you is that you're different, and you don't even know it," she would preach at me, shaking her head slightly as if it was a shame I was keeping myself so small. Sam herself strode through campus and social events brazenly, like she knew her rightful destination and was on her way to it. I considered this when I watched the way she moved through the room. I wanted to be that bold; I hated being so fearful of getting life all wrong. And there was Sam, modeling such confidence and inviting me to come along. She was teaching me how to break out of my bubble. For the first time, I questioned all of my strict rules, all of the boundaries I'd created in order to feel safe and gain approval. She was teaching me, through her own freedom, how to be free myself.

When I decided, just shy of turning twenty-one, that I wanted to try alcohol for the first time, of course I called Sam. We met at a friend's house with a paper bag concealing illicit contents. Sam and Jenny made a big deal of me crossing this threshold, while at the same time not making me self-conscious. I think they always knew I would decide to buck all my built-in systems, and I think they both wanted to be there when I did.

When I decided, just shy of twenty-two, to have sex for the first time, in a deliberate and overwrought decision, I again called Sam. After class, we drove to the parking lot of a campus bar and parked beside the dumpster while I explained, slowly, my plight. I took big, gulping breaths. The late afternoon light bounced off the warm concrete, and we had to pull the shades down to block the harshness. She stared forward out the window and gave me explicit instructions. Later, she pointedly did not follow up. I've never told anyone this story.

My friendship with Sam began to change as our lives diverged after college. At first, we wrote long, rambling daily emails about how we were faring in the real world. I sent her messages from a movie set; she replied from a corporate cubicle. We continued to see one another a few times a year, but that eventually dwindled to a girls' trip with other sorority sisters each spring. We got married just one month apart, bridesmaids for one another in tulle and satin. Our paths spread wider, and where our opposite natures had once been what made us compatible, as time went on, it made us combustible.

There is so much I could say about my friendship with Sam, and about its eventual demise. In the end, we both got some things wrong about each other. There are some days I wish I could take back. It occurs to me now that she could fit into any of these chapters, really. But I'm choosing to write about her here, in the question about who taught me how to be. Sam was there when my worldview first expanded; she was there when I took my first baby steps out of the trap of being "good" and turned in the direction of being "true." She commanded me to fly, saw it through, and then she let me go.

• • •

Yasmin showed up at book club, a spinoff of the original book club I had started years before. This was a new group, and from the start, I felt like an outsider. I brought my love of dark novels into a book club full of activists and advocates, women educated on social justice and loud about their political leanings.

Yasmin intimidated me right off the bat. She wore her curly hair big, and her face was striking in its beauty. Her experiences, including growing up Muslim and spending years abroad living in Paris, were beyond anything I could relate to. When she offered up opinions or referenced material in our discussions, she was often citing feminist heroes I'd never heard of or racial history I was profoundly ignorant of. I had to bluff my way through some of those conversations.

I kept going to the meetings, though. It was stimulating to be out of my usual bubble. These women were funny and interesting, and they gave me a lot to think about. A few months after the book club began, at the heart of the holiday season, we were sitting around a kitchen table with coffee and pastries and the subject of Angel Trees came up, the charity-based practice of buying presents for strangers who otherwise might not have any gifts for their children on Christmas morning. Someone brought up a program that had a more personal approach, where you adopted a family for Christmas and then delivered the gifts and food yourself. This organization was less about charity and more about bridge-building. I expressed hesitation at this idea, and went into a long-winded explanation of not wanting to feel like a white savior, not wanting to pat myself on the back, not wanting to put the recipients in a face-to-face situation of gratitude. I thought, in all sincerity, that I was being compassionate and empathetic, sensitive to the shame that must surround the person in need.

Yasmin leveled her eyes at me from across the table and said calmly, "Now that is some white people shit right there."

Her tone wasn't malicious, but her words stung. Yasmin, a person of color, had been slowly educating me in every conversation we had. It wasn't explicit, but she seemed to sense that I was willing and eager to learn more about race and was too polite to outright ask for help understanding. The holiday conversation opened a whole new dialogue between us. Help is help, she said. Withholding help because of your own mind swirl is unhelpful.

I needed to know more. It felt like every time I started to get the hang of being an ally of social reform, Yasmin pivoted. She was adept at upholding both sides of any argument, and she led me by the nose through each obstacle until I understood more clearly what I actually believed about race and history and equality—and how much I *didn't* know about black people in America. We established a trust between us. She came to see that my questions came from a sincere place, from a desire to understand, and I grew less afraid of her candor and gentle reproaches.

Yasmin taught me how to talk about hard things with a friend. I learned to listen to her experience without getting defensive or offering a pat solution. She showed me how to read between the lines of everything from news reports to legislation, and to think about how they affect people without all of my advantages.

After we'd been in book club for a couple of years, having conversations so rich I often wished I had recorded them,

Yasmin approached me about taking these conversations public on my podcast. At the time, I was producing and hosting a show I called *Smartest Person in the Room*, a series of deep dives and interviews with experts on various subjects. Yasmin wanted to do one about race.

I balked. I was, at book club, the whitest person in the room, and if I'd learned anything at all, it was that we were living in an age of listening to people of color, and my job was to sit down and shut up. The optics of a white-person-led conversation about race amid the Ferguson protests and regular headlines about police brutality felt like a bad idea. Not to mention terrifying.

But Yasmin pressed. "You have an audience," she said, "an audience of white people who need to hear these things and who will listen if it comes from you."

I demurred for months, my own fear keeping me from seeing any value in talking about race publicly. I had a history of playing it safe on the internet. I'd really had only one big kerfuffle during my blogging heyday, and it was, not ironically, about race. I had misstepped in that instance and had never really forgiven myself for it. I knew that incident was tiny compared to the bag of worms I'd be opening if I did a race series on the podcast.

But the headlines kept coming. And my own reading and self-education, aided mostly by Yasmin, was making me understand that it is absolutely the job of the majority to educate others within the majority. I didn't have many white friends who had a Yasmin in their lives, someone to speak frankly with them about their experiences in the world, the fear they lived with, and why.

With trepidation, I recorded our first conversation together, a rehash in broad strokes of all the things Yasmin and I had been discussing privately for over a year. Off mic, I told her I was scared to make the series.

"Why?" she asked.

"I'm scared of Twitter trolls," I said. "I'm scared of messing this up. The stakes are high."

"For who, white girl?"

I knew she was right. So what if someone came after me on Twitter? People of color in the United States are living in fear of their lives.

And if I did misstep with my words or mangled my stated intentions? If I trusted a fallible human or alienated half my audience? Well, I would survive that. And the upside would be that in having these conversations publicly, maybe I would learn enough to impart an important message. Maybe what I viewed as risky wasn't risky in actuality. Maybe it would move the needle just the tiniest direction toward freedom and equality. Wasn't that worth it, to stand on this side of history? Yasmin gave me clarity about what's important, what's worth it. Yasmin taught me how to be, with a platform.

The six-part series titled "Racial Bias: Conversations Between Friends" aired on my podcast through the spring and summer of 2018, and while it wasn't without criticism, I did not face the onslaught I was expecting. I never, ever would have made that race series without Yasmin's urging, without her seeing the potential for it and pushing me beyond my comfort zone. That podcast series, while not perfect, was listened to by tens of thousands of people. Maybe they learned something. Maybe they took one of the points to a friend for a conversation. Maybe it changed the way they read the news. I hope so. Because making that show, in collaboration with a friend who was teaching me how to be a better advocate for my fellow humans, certainly changed me.

Your Turn

So, who taught you how to be? Who taught you how to act, and how to grow? Who are your Auntie Mames, your society ladies, your Sam, your Yasmin?

Think about your family of origin and the messages that were imparted by your parents and siblings. In good and bad ways, how did they model actions and attitudes that you took on without noticing?

If it's easier to think about who influenced you as a child, but you're drawing a blank on who infiltrates your thoughts as an adult, here are a few things to think about:

Who in your social circle do/did you admire and take every opportunity to be around? Likely that person is teaching you some way to be. I have friends with impeccable style and taste, and I enjoy being in their presence and in their homes because they give me ideas for how to decorate and how to dress. They make me want to look for the beauty in everyday things and to shop my own closet for something to wear that will be a perfect expression of myself.

Similarly, I know moms who blow me away with their grace and patience in parenting. When they tell me how they handled a disciplinary issue, or how they're thinking about a big decision with their kids, my ears perk up. They can teach me something with a simple text.

What thought leaders are shaping your perspective on the news and current events, on personal growth, or even on pop culture? Who we follow online affects us enormously. If you're like me, you don't want this to be true. We want to think we've curated our feeds for fun or that we are capable of our own opinions, thank you very much. But I've watched the most educated people I know parrot a talking point or joke. Sometimes we aren't even sure how we feel about something until we see a particularly well-articulated point and then we think, *That! That is how I feel about this!*

Fessing up that we can learn from online listicles and memes doesn't have to feel humiliating. Just be aware of it. Who do you follow who makes you think? Or makes you add a dress to your online shopping cart? Or has a certain spin on current events that resonates with you? We are all teaching one another online. You don't have to give a TED talk to have an effect on the way someone sees an issue. In fact, I might give more weight to my neighbor's thoughtful opinion than to a stranger's.

Don't lie to yourself by pretending you're so unique a soul as to not take on the traits of others, or that you don't have the power to influence others. We are all being shaped daily, indirectly and unconsciously. Yes, we have a core self that contains its own moral compass, its own tastes and direction that are independent of our noisy world. But it's impossible not to be influenced. We are attracted and repelled by all sorts of trains of thought, all sorts of people and art and activity. I'd like to think that the things we move toward are a reflection of ourselves or of the selves we want to be. As adults, we have the choice to move away from the opposite things: the people who are teaching us who we *don't* want to be.

As you're thinking about who taught you how to be, turn it around for just a minute and realize who YOU are teaching how to be. The first thought that comes to my mind is of my children, of course, and how my husband and I are teaching them how to be in the world every day through our own words and actions. But we also influence friends and acquaintances all the time. Our interactions and posts matter. Ideally, our online selves are a reflection of what we're like in person, with as much grace and manners as we would muster if we gathered all of our online "friends" into our personal living rooms.

Every day, someone is teaching us how to be, and we're teaching someone else how to be. Pull out a notebook and start to list the people who have influenced you throughout your life. Don't overthink it. Don't edit. Don't try to put it in order. Include fictional characters and celebrities from the books, movies, music, and TV shows you've loved. Think about who you wanted to imitate in style, appearance, talent, and leadership.

Once you have your list, look at it as a whole. Is there a theme? Can you sense what you took on as part of your identity and what you shed like a hot potato? Does it make you laugh? Does it make you cringe? If so, good. There's no shame in admitting you've been influenced. It's happening to all of us, all the time. The hope is that we just get better at who we follow and admire. I mean, I used to want to look like Kelly Kapowski. I don't anymore. That's GROWTH.

Notable Fashion Choices

1. When I was seven or eight, I had a pair of denim knickers—almost like pantaloons—that I wore constantly. They were not cute. They were a little Dickensian. Once, when I was wearing them, a friend's mom told me I dressed like a ragamuffin, and I was furious.

2. I designed my own senior prom dress for the disco-themed dance. I picked out three colors of bright satin, and my mom created a gorgeous, color-block gown.

3. When I was a college student studying abroad in England, I stumbled across a tiny little thrift store about the size of a closet in an alleyway in London. I picked out a vintage '70s belted suede coat for about $40, a big splurge at the time. I wore it and cherished it for years after. I still have it.

4. I spent a good chunk of time in college crimping my short, choppy Meg Ryan haircut with a crimping iron, which made it poof out frizzily in all directions. I think I was hoping for volume and drama, but it actually just looked ridiculous.

5. After living in California for about a year, in a desperate move to further reinvent myself, I dyed my light blonde hair a deep, inky black. I was going for Cher, but it was quite a bit more vampire. The color was unflattering, to say the least, and I eventually let it fade, but it did what I needed it to do: served as a delineation between one stage of my life and the next.

6. Also during that first year in LA, I was gifted my first pair of designer jeans. Well, not exactly gifted. They were given to me in lieu of payment for babysitting, and I cannot remember a more creative form of payment. The friend I was babysitting for took

me to a fancy department store and let me try on pair after pair of denim until I landed on a faded pair of Seven for all Mankind. It was better than cash.

7. My wedding dress made me feel so beautiful. I'd always imagined myself in a big tulle ballgown, but when it came time to choose, I actually decided upon a slim, trumpet silhouette with an intricate lace overlay. It will forever be my most favorite fashion decision.

8. After my babies were born, in an effort to "get back to myself," I went on a pink spree. We painted our living room pink. I dyed the ends of my blonde hair pink. I bought pink pants and a pink blazer, and it was a real Elle Woods moment. Actually, this might be a phase I'm still in.

9. I have dozens of sweatshirts. I'm easily chilled, and I work from home, so my go-to daily outfit often involves a sweatshirt. On the style scale, mine range from boring hoodie to trendy and bold. One day, I posted online about a knockoff sweatshirt design at Walmart, and the #sweatshirtcult hashtag was born. I do not want to be in charge of a sweatshirt cult, but we should all lead with our strengths.

10. Three of my best friends and I bought ourselves grown-up friendship bracelets. Together we took a trip to the jewelry store and chose four delicate bracelets, each with different colored stones. I love looking down at my wrist and seeing this symbol of friendship and love. (Side note: when I turned in the first draft of this book, these same friends took me to the same jewelry store in celebration to pick out a little commemorative piece. It's so nice to have traditions and milestone markers with people.)

Chapter

SIX

When Did You Belong?

The differences between the seasons when you felt you belonged and those when you felt like an outsider can be stark. Our emotional cup is filled to the brim when we feel like we fit and are loved by our family, friends, and community. In contrast, the times when we felt unwelcome or like we were kept out of the circle can stand out as periods of isolation and rejection. It's also true that we can simultaneously belong in one area but not in another, and that becomes an emotional juggling act. We belong in our families, but not at school, or vice versa. We no longer fit in our churches, but have found like-mindedness in our yoga classes.

This feeling of belonging is not always all or nothing. The belonging I found online when I started blogging didn't erase the pervasive discomfort I felt every day that I didn't fully belong in my new roles as a wife and mother. We have to feel like we belong SOMEWHERE in order to feel whole in our relationships, in our belief systems, in our callings.

It's funny, but when I first sat down to make a list of the places, groups, and relationships where I felt I truly belonged,

101

I conjured some beautiful, defining memories. At the same time, I could see that I no longer belong in some of those places. Not only because of my age and life experiences, but because I've evolved from the girl who felt most at home in these spaces of conformity. In some cases, I now stand in opposition to the very things that I claimed made those things so special back then.

Still, I can hold all these contradictions in my story at once. There are places where I once belonged that informed my worldview in a way that was largely positive for my soul at that time. But as life moved forward, I changed and no longer felt at home in those communities. Looking back, I know now that only a sliver of the belonging was about the institution it was built around. It was always about the people.

Belonging is always about people.

I'll Go First

It was without irony that my non-religious parents sent shy, anxious, non-sportsy me to the radically evangelical athletic summer camp for four weeks each year. My older siblings had gone before me, and I wasn't given a choice. Every summer, my mom and dad shipped me off to the beautiful Ozark mountains for daily instruction in sports and Jesus.

Objectively speaking, camp should not have been my thing. I was an introverted kid who was used to hours of alone time each day, and the ten bunks in each rugged cabin made that impossible. I didn't like to run; I especially didn't like team competition, and that was exactly the focus of our days, with only the occasional arts and crafts or nature class thrown in. When we arrived, we had to turn over any books that were not explicitly Christian. At seven years old, I did not read religious books, so I had to hand over the stacks of *Sweet Valley Twins* and *The Babysitter's Club* that I had packed for the long bus ride.

I cannot imagine what my parents were thinking when they sent me there, other than it was a popular place to send kids and gave them a brief reprieve as working parents faced with a long summer. They surely also must have seen that camp would be good for me, in all the ways that camp is good for most kids: it teaches independence, fosters a sense of adventure, and was a crash course in the moral and religious teachings I was already picking up through general Bible Belt culture.

For each of those ten summers, I was a happy camper. I belonged at camp as I never had before (and maybe never will again). The camp itself put a lot of emphasis on belonging, despite never using that term. They taught us that everyone had a place, and everyone was valued. Camp felt like heaven on earth to me; I couldn't imagine anywhere I would rather be, at any time, than at camp.

What gave the place such a strong sense of belonging? For one thing, everyone looked like me. The other campers came from families similar to mine, with professional parents in preppy clothes who mostly voted the same way. I felt I belonged because they told me that the Bible said I did, and this, more than anything else, appealed to me. The notion that I was chosen, for this life and this path, soothed me. It wasn't until later that I realized that if this was indeed true, many people on earth must have been "picked" for a less fortunate path.

At camp, I was the fullest expression of myself. At camp I could be loud or quiet. I could boisterously cheer on my team and clumsily try to get the ball—all my efforts were not only accepted but celebrated. At camp, I danced, I ran, I canoed. I moved muscles that were dormant the other eleven months of the year. And every day, I felt I was in the exact right place at the exact right time. My feet were rooted to the ground. I was happy to be alive.

My sense of belonging at camp morphed and deepened over the years. In the beginning, it was about fitting in, knowing the culture of the camp, the humor, the rules. Each morning dawned with children in line at the flagpole, with a salute followed by a prayer; and each day ended in that kind of exhaustion you only feel when you're a kid. Limbs tired from swimming and swinging and clapping. Heart full from laughing and making spiritual connections with peers. Brain buzzing from new concepts and intense instruction. It was all so exhilarating.

As I got older, my sense of belonging derived from camp, it being the one place where I was living with people who shared my beliefs about God and the Bible, and this upped the stakes for me. Most of the year, I would cling to my Bible, afraid that I would make a misstep, but at camp I could loosen my grip. I was among friends. Someone else was keeping us on eternal task.

I belonged at camp because I attended for so long. Many of the campers I met those first few summers stopped coming by the time they entered high school. Only a handful of us kept showing up each year, and we were respected for our leather necklaces gleaming with trinkets that announced our seniority. A bird was gifted for year three, a fish for year eight. This was the only jewelry allowed, and mine bore the highest marks.

I belonged at camp because I loved camp. The sermons preached in the simple, sawdust-strewn chapel shaped my worldview. But I also belonged because I blindly believed. At the time, that was good enough for camp, and for me. I didn't question anything I learned about Jesus or the Bible or how to be "good" in the eyes of the Lord, because for a long time, camp was my only authority on the matter. It wasn't until years later, when I could better suss out the more harmful messages about lust and spousal submission (to teenagers!) that I realized maybe I didn't believe everything they were telling me to believe.

● ● ●

When it came down to it, I didn't want to go to college at all. I was sick of school and had spent the last two years of high school devising ways to take fewer classes. So the idea of college—which had always been pitched to me as rigorous and liberal, a place where you had to stand your ground and resist outside thought—didn't appeal to me in any way. It seemed hard and unnecessary to the only career I envisioned for myself: as a writer (oh, how silly and know-it-all I was then!). My parents rejected each and every reason I gave for why I didn't need to go to college. Their belief in higher education was a tenet in our family. They cared about it; they championed it. It didn't occur to me that my parents wanted to provide a better education than what I was getting in my small public high school in a state ranked forty-seventh in the nation for education. I didn't connect the dots that after a senior year of health challenges and emotional roller coasters, the safety net of college might be the softest place to land. At the height of my entitlement, I rolled my eyes, took their gift of a debt-free college education, and high-tailed it up the interstate to the University of Oklahoma.

I chose the same major my older sister had chosen at the same school where both of our parents were alumni. Many of my high school classmates would also be at OU. What I'm saying here is it wasn't a unique path. Lacking any better ideas, I was rolling down the highway of obligations and expectations, and the one emotional off-ramp was sorority rush. Greek life felt like somewhere I could really distinguish myself. Being in a sorority would give me instant community and a reason to leave my dorm room. For the first time, I felt like I had a choice in this part of my future. By choosing the letters on my shirt, I would set the tone for the next four years.

Now, let me just stop here for a moment to acknowledge the legitimate criticisms of sorority rush and female standards of beauty and exclusivity and the horrifying gauntlet of "cutting" girls who "don't fit." An alternate version of this section exists, one wherein I rail against the fact that co-eds are told they do not belong, and for the worst, most superficial reasons. Because of this, I thought about leaving this story out, playing it safe by not writing chirpily about my college sorority days. But pledging Theta was what kept me in college. Living with and being in communion with 200 other women cracked the world's door open for me just a little bit more. Maybe it could have happened in college (or in life) another way, but it didn't. Our stories and our life experiences are steeped in these disclaimers of, "Well, I feel kind of different about this now."

So I'm going to tell you now about how being in an elitist girls' club with creepy rituals turned out to be good for me. How belonging in this sisterhood taught me how to be comfortable in groups of women.

At a school as big as OU, there were more than a dozen options to choose from. Potential pledges walk through each sorority house looking for one of two things: somewhere they belong, or somewhere they WANT to belong.

This is who I am, or *this is who I want to be.*

For me, choosing a sorority was the latter. I enjoyed the process, but when I walked into the Theta house, I felt out of my league. The girls on the little makeshift stage were beautiful; they sparkled, and their skits involved complicated harmonious singing. Their vibe during rush week was less cutesy and more classy. They weren't cheerleaders; they were charity-ball-throwers. I took one look at this roomful of women, most of them only a year or two older than I was, and we seemed worlds apart. And I wanted to be worlds apart from who I was. I looked wrong. I said the wrong things. I didn't know how to dress or how to speak well. I never thought they'd take me, but I knew I'd regret it if I didn't try.

On the last morning of rush, a letter was slipped under my door. Up and down the dorm hallways, there were tears and shrieks. When I opened the envelope and out fell an embossed card with a black-and-gold crest, I stared at it in disbelief. I felt like it was a mistake. Suddenly, I was terrified. Because I didn't REALLY belong there, and somehow I'd tricked them into believing I did. This was thrilling, and I took it all seriously, arming myself in the only way I knew how: by assimilating.

During my time as a Theta, I started to look more and more like my sorority sisters. My hair got blonder, my lipstick brighter. My clothes became indistinguishable from any of my roommates' clothes. I tamed my unibrow.

I realize I'm describing what sounds like death to individuality, but conforming to one standard gave me the confidence to break all those rules down the road. All 200 of us wore a uniform of sorts—not mandated, just chosen—of sorority t-shirts and loose-fitting shorts or pants for class, tight black pants and shimmery tops for nights out. This was the '90s after all, and our style was simple and the same, and it leveled the playing field for someone who was still figuring out how to play the game. Living in a sorority enabled me to watch other girls my age slowly become women right before my very eyes.

Like any microcosm, the sorority included girls who were natural leaders and those who couldn't help but rebel. There were business majors and art students. Most impressively, there was the contingent who ran the house like a tight ship, and I admired how so many strong-minded women could live in relative harmony, contributing regularly on campus and in philanthropy, presiding over interpersonal discipline commit-tees. We threw parties and entered national competitions, and everyone was involved in choosing the new members each year. All the while, we were making grades and sending successful women out into the world. This well-oiled machine was effi-cient and productive, and I couldn't have learned half as much through real-world experience as I learned from these women in this contrived situation.

On graduation day, when I stood on the sorority house lawn in my cap and gown, I knew that out of everything I had learned and would remember about college, my classes had had the least impact on the person I had become. Theta was the institution that gave me the most tools for life. The sorority taught me the importance of quality leadership and how to live in community. As a sisterhood, we kept one another safe and offered more grace than is often found in the culture at large.

I belonged as a Theta because I was most comfortable with conformity. That would change, but not immediately. Those women made me feel safe, and I hope I extended my own net of safety around them in turn. That, then, was belonging.

●　●　●

We ate outside, underneath string lights, because it was summer in Los Angeles. At the table were about a dozen friends, including a fresh LA transplant my new husband had just hired to work for his production company. Jeff invited Priya to the celebration because she was new to the city, and he was sure she and I would get along. Priya ended up across the table, and because it's always a natural starting point for me, we shared the books we'd been reading. Priya was sharp and curious; she had a breadth of literary knowledge that I craved in a friend. Not long into our conversation, I said, half-jokingly, "We should start a book club!" And her face lit up.

It was one of those sentences that could have been a polite throwaway, offered with the best of intentions but never followed up on. Instead, our book club became a place to belong and the thing that would carry me through that stage of my life.

By the middle of the summer, we had an email chain going and a book selected. I reached out to a former roommate, Rachel, and she forwarded the email to her best friend, Nora. The four of us—me, Priya, Rachel, and Nora—were the founding members. We had never been in a book club, so we made up the rules as we went. We met once a month at our homes, rotating who hosted, and the host picked the book we read. We chose Sunday mornings as our designated meeting time. As the months went on, we added two more women.

We met regularly and for hours at a time. We started around brunch and often didn't leave our seats until mid-afternoon.

We almost always read the book—there was real nerd-shaming if you didn't—and took the literary discussion seriously. But the other hours were full of something I hadn't found in Los Angeles until this group formed.

When we started book club, I had recently quit my job in television production and was overseeing the repair and renovation of our 1920s home while trying to get pregnant. It was not where I had thought I would be as I approached thirty, but it's where I was. I loved my husband, and I wanted a family, but I went days without seeing another human besides Jeff, who was busy in a thriving career, making a new movie and multiple TV shows. It was a middle place for me, to be out of a job but not yet a mother. Sometimes book club was the only social thing I did all month. It was impossible to hold that lightly. The very first novel we read was about talking dogs, and even though I kind of hated it, I have never been able to part with my copy.

Book club was an oasis. We talked about our childhoods and work and relationships and dreams. We got into the deep stuff, and we shared it boldly, learning early on to trust one another with our struggles and wishes.

Book club—we never bothered to give it a better name—was a lifesaver, and our deep and lively conversations broadened my mind. We were Jewish and Christian and atheist. We were activists and peacemakers. We grew up in California, New York, Oklahoma, and New Jersey. They were a range of liberal, and I fell on the conservative side. We were learning from one another with every single meeting. The books we read drew out our values, our tastes, and our differences.

By circumstances not necessarily designed, we didn't see each other socially outside of our monthly meetings. Our interaction stayed in this bubble of warmth and croissants and occasional mimosas, where we shared our current heartaches or triumphs. We all seemed to understand, without spelling it out, that we had created something sacred.

We met every month for years. There were weddings, job changes, movies made, books released, and, eventually, babies. We read memoirs and novels and mysteries. We rarely all agreed on a book.

One fall, after we'd been meeting for many years, after we'd seen one another through several evolutions of the mind, body, and spirit, Rachel announced that she was moving her little family of four to Oakland. Not long after, Nora told us she was moving back to New York City. Book club came to a natural end. It had buoyed me through my loneliest years, and I was devastated when it was over.

The women in my book club genuinely accepted me when I was an obvious work in progress. We all experienced growth from our friendship, but I had started as the odd one out, politically, religiously, and literarily. And their perspectives— which were never full of scorn or dismissiveness when we disagreed—had opened my mind and heart over and over. I think we were all a little more gentle at dinner parties after that, as book club taught us not to assume anything about what another person believes or feels.

Book club ended just about the time that I met another group of women who would teach me a great deal. I'd like to think I was handed off from one caring female nest into another. I'm not sure if I would have had the courage or the authority to be in such a dynamic if I hadn't had book club first, and a sisterhood before that.

● ● ●

The internet might sound like an unlikely place to find belonging, but it offered that for me after I started my mommy blog. It was just a few months after Lucy was born, and I'd been reading blogs religiously before I decided to make a go of it myself.

Writing for an audience who offered immediate feedback was gratifying, and I spent those long days of early motherhood thinking about what I was going to write, writing it in one draft, and then responding to readers in the comments section. It was a feedback loop that would come to define the internet, but before it took a dark turn, the interaction was like manna for all the new moms at home, covered in spit up and wondering if we'd ever be back to ourselves.

Pouring out my heart online led to real-life Twitter meetups and, eventually, conferences focused on bloggers. Finally, after years of friendship stops and starts in Los Angeles, I was meeting my people. They were out there; I just needed a hashtag to find them.

After one of those blogger conferences, I received an invitation to join a small Facebook group created for like-minded bloggers. Blogs were booming, and Facebook felt like a safe space at the time (#naive). At first the group was just twenty random women with not much else in common besides the fact that we knew our way around SEO keywords, and we had a loose association with faith. Maybe both of those things were a little shaky from the start. We were from all across North America, the farthest in Canada, in California, Utah, and down through Tennessee and Alabama. We weren't all married, and we weren't all mothers.

It's impossible to say why some groups have a magical chemistry and some don't. There are too many possible factors and layers. If pressed, I would say the thing that bonded us together initially was timing. We were all lonely in our own ways, and we were all in front of our screens most of the day. So what followed was a never-ending thread of chat. From work cubicles, from playrooms, from three different time zones and three different decades of life, we talked about everything. We were in a rush to get it all out—everything we'd been storing in our hearts for our entire adult lives. We told our love stories and our biggest fears. We were, collectively, so funny that more than once, I found myself typing back to someone through tears of laughter. It was the honeymoon of friendship.

I belonged in this group because they told me I did. They claimed me. We claimed one another. Not since the sorority house had I felt such a certain knowing of my place in the world, a place that we created. Our online friendship became real-life friendship, and I now consider these women I first met through a computer screen to be my lifetime ride-or-dies. They let me show up as the real me during a time when I was consumed with my online image. It was the reality check and camaraderie I needed, and often still need.

Your Turn

Those are my stories about belonging. Now it's time for you to think about the times in your life when you belonged. If that feeling has become unfamiliar to you, maybe tap back into the memories of when you last belonged somewhere, and see where you can apply a similar circumstance to your life right now.

You might also think about when you felt out of place. Were there times when your family or community felt like an itchy sweater? Have you ever suddenly surveyed the relationship landscape and thought, *I do not belong here*. What stories do you have to tell about that?

It likely feels a bit disconcerting to think about the times when you didn't belong.

For me, not belonging gave way to anxiety and self-doubt. I questioned my ability to be a good friend and felt there was something wrong with me for not fitting in—because I could see that there was nothing wrong with the women in the group or the group itself. I see now that this is a twisted way to think about relationships. It's okay to not fit in, because we can't fit in everywhere and be true to who we are. It's okay that my personality and my path were different, but I couldn't see it objectively at the time. I was feeling unsteady in other areas of my life, and I took those emotions and misapplied them to a situation where I simply didn't fit in, causing me to feel isolated and scrambling for equilibrium. Especially when I no longer belonged in a place where I had belonged previously. That didn't feel like growth. It felt like rejection.

When did you belong? Where do you belong still? Have there been times of un-belonging? If so, how do you look back on that now? Perhaps you're in the middle of figuring this all out—if you are, that's okay; you *will* figure it out. And then, down the line, you might have to figure it out again. But you'll know better the next time, and then again the next. You'll be less likely to self-flagellate and more likely to see that you won't always belong. Also, belonging is a wonderful thing, so you'd better get to it.

Ways to Journal

I will sing from the highest hills how transformative journaling can be, but I understand that not everyone knows where to start or how to think about it outside of the traditional journal idea. But there are ways for every personality type to document events and emotions.

1. Dear Diary

   This happened.
   This is how I felt about it.

2. Bullet lists

   Everything I remember about vacation:
   - *It rained.*
   - *We took a bike tour with a wacky guide named Henry.*
   - *Lucy & Finch snorkeled for the first time!*

3. One sentence a day

   We needed to get out of the house, so we went to the park and tried to forget about our stupid fight over the dog from earlier (it worked).

4. Stream of consciousness

   (Hat tip to Julia Cameron's Morning Pages idea in her book *The Artist's Way*.)

5. Intuitive journaling

   Ask yourself a question at the top of the page, sit with your intuition for a moment, then write down whatever comes up without questioning it. The act of writing will sometimes unblock whatever your emotions are protecting you from.

6. Affirmation journaling

Writing kind words to yourself in the hope that your soul will start to believe them.

- *I am a joyful person.*
- *I am happy and strong in my body.*

7. Using an app to journal on your phone

There are a number of these to choose from that will help you keep track of your thoughts and activities using the one thing you most likely always have with you: your phone.

8. Keeping a long word processing document on your computer

I believe something special happens when we use a pen and paper, and that our own handwriting transmits emotion more than we think, but I also accept that we're living in a digital world, and many people are most comfortable typing. If you have a lot to say and feel like writing it down would take too long or take too much effort, keep a document on your computer where you can easily access it, and type your thoughts and feelings.

9. Multi-person journaling

This can be a really interesting aspect of a relationship: writing down feelings or events in a shared journal. Often, people might be able to write something down they would never be able to speak, so it can become a place for mutually expressed emotion.

10. Video journaling

If speaking is within your comfort level but writing longhand or digitally is not, consider keeping a video journal.

Chapter
SEVEN

When Did
It Change?

Some events are so transformational that if you were to look back at a map of your life, they would be marked by a sign with an arrow and the words Sharp Turn Here. Sometimes life changes because of a traumatic event: a death, a divorce, a layoff, or a natural disaster. Other times it's the little things in your everyday that tip off a change that was already building within you: seeing a disappointing photo of yourself that leads to a lifestyle overhaul; overhearing what a friend really thinks about you.

I think most of us have a collection of these types of stories, the big and little things that necessitated a reroute. The few stories of change I'm going to share here don't revolve around life's greatest hardships, but they are moments when my life shifted course. They don't fit into a typical narrative where you might expect a major life change to occur.

This is exactly why I like to keep a journal: because we don't always know we're in the middle of a major moment until the ground beneath us shifts. My journal allows me to go back over the events and emotions I've documented so that I can identify *those moments. And when something major does happen, when I already know things will never be the same, I have a record of my thoughts and feelings in real time. If you're not a journaler, don't worry. I'm sure you can still recount the times when your path took a detour.*

These are the few stories of change from my life that have withstood the test of time.

I'll Go First

Fred and I dated for four years, from our junior year in high school until our sophomore year in college. Our relationship made sense in our small town, but we were ill-matched to take on the world. Fred was quiet and focused and made things with his hands: large speakers, custom furniture. He was somehow both preppy and rugged, wearing low-key designer clothes before guys did that so obviously. His flannel, hi-tech camping boots, and taste in cars were more suited to Colorado than Oklahoma.

At sixteen, I was an obnoxious know-it-all. I talked down to my teachers and to everyone else. I laughed hard and often, had a selfish streak a mile wide, and the inkling to move far away from my place of upbringing, though I hadn't named it yet. I was restless and superior.

Fred was quietly alpha, the envy of guys and girls alike, and I was a wannabe alpha who parroted the books I read as if they were original thoughts. Fred and I were very different but saw ourselves as outliers in a regimented community. I think we recognized an innocent rebellion in one another.

I forget now what love is like when you're sixteen. My journals tell me there were lots of ups and downs, including one spectacularly bad prom situation. Fred and I had a pattern of breaking up and getting back together in a dramatic fashion. But after three years together, we were like an old married couple. There weren't many surprises left. We felt safe. We made one another laugh. He tracked our relationship by making monthly calendars with an original drawing on each new page. One summer he burned me a mixed CD and dubbed his own voice over the bad words in our favorite songs, so I could play it without worry. For Valentine's Day, I made him a set of cards detailing each line of the Proverbs 31 Bible verse about godly women (how romantic!).

Fred and I had been a couple for so long that there was a lot of enmeshment. We had the same friends, the same values, shared the same high school memories, and we'd brought a lot of that sameness to college. We were growing up, but each still clung to the familiarity the other offered.

On the weekends, we frequently made the drive between our college town and our hometown together, taking his SUV the two hours down the interstate. It was fine just to have one car between us. Our parents lived in adjacent neighborhoods.

One Saturday night, we were parked in my parents' driveway, making out in his car. Things got heated, and I don't mean the seats. I made a verbal jab, and he spit it back at me. Somehow, we were making out and fighting at the same time. I threatened something, and he sat in stony silence. At some point, we retreated to our separate sides of the car. Eventually, Fred said something breathtakingly hurtful. I can't remember the details, but I remember it stunned us both. I could read on his face that he regretted it instantly.

We ended on this nasty note, and I slammed the car door and stomped inside the house. I was shocked by how the evening had taken a turn, but a part of me felt the release of exploded passion. I watched from the front windows as he peeled out of the driveway and down the street toward his own home. I noted that he kept his eyes straight ahead, not glancing back toward the house, where he surely surmised I was watching.

I wobbled to the bathroom to cry and think about how to proceed. We hadn't fought like that in a long time. I wasn't exactly sure of the rules, but I knew we wouldn't go long without making up. I couldn't even believe he'd made it out of the driveway without turning around. When my shaking subsided, I went back out to the porch to wait.

I just knew he was going to come back. For one thing, he was my ride back to the college. But really, it was our fight that should have sent him speeding back to my arms. We'd both been wrong. We never let things just hang.

An hour passed. Each time headlights bounced around the curve of the road, I held my breath. It was never Fred.

I went inside for the few minutes it took to grab a quilt out of the closet. I wrapped it tightly around me, and curled up cross-legged on the stone bench in front of the house. I watched the road for hours. My dad came outside to check on me once but didn't ask many questions. He nodded silently at my terseness and went back in. When I finally crawled into bed in my teenage room, under my old heartthrob posters, it was well after midnight, and the tears were long dried on my face.

Fred didn't call until late the next afternoon, and then only to make obligatory arrangements for the drive back to school. I'd already asked my parents to drive me and didn't explain how I'd lost my ride.

"Where did you go last night?" I asked. I didn't sound casual, but I was humiliated at how long I'd waited.

"I took my mom to the movies," he said.

Oh.

I'll never forget how I felt sitting wrapped in that quilt on the porch for hours. My little cold feet. How I didn't even leave my post for bathroom breaks for fear I'd miss a drive-by. Fred hadn't been staring out the window looking up at the same stars, contemplating our future and feeling sorry about our fight. He wasn't thinking about me at all. He'd taken his mom to the movies. He was ordering extra butter on his popcorn and zoning out.

Fred and I limped along for a few more months, but later, I could point back to that night as the beginning of the end. I'm still not sure why that moment was the one that made me realize love wasn't supposed to look like my relationship with Fred. He was a good person, but we were not good together. Our fight that night wasn't the worst disagreement we ever had, but it was one of the last. Whether it was ego or justice or something else, I swore I would never let Fred or anyone else make me feel that abandoned, that disillusioned, that pathetic. I would never again rearrange myself for someone who wasn't thinking about me at all.

(*Postscript*: Okay, so I did make a similar pitiful mistake one more time, and only a few years after Fred. But when my head cleared, and I realized I was metaphorically waiting on a porch for someone who wasn't coming back, I vowed *never again* anew. Sometimes you end up mucking it up twice. But it's the first time that sticks with you.)

●　●　●

One conversation with my oldest friend, Drew, is responsible for flicking the domino that caused every other piece to topple in my wobbly constructed faith.

I remember exactly where I was standing when Drew told me he was gay. We were on the phone, me at a babysitting job in Los Angeles, and he in an apartment in Oklahoma. He didn't use words. It was the long silences, heavy sighs, and finally the sobs that I'd never heard come from him before that told me what he couldn't actually tell me. Drew and I were both in our mid-twenties and had been friends since we were children. When he called me that night, I couldn't have known it was going to be a conversation that changed us both.

I was the first person Drew told his big secret, but I wasn't the first person to know. We can belly laugh now about how this musical-loving, girl-best-friends-only, singing, dancing, leaping young boy was the picture of a gay cliché. But it was the middle of the Bible Belt in a time when assuming someone was anything but heterosexual was to damn them to hell. And so we just did not address it.

Drew learned to hide his pain well. He was the life of every party, a natural performer, and an adept deflector. I wondered why he never coupled off while the rest of us experimented throughout adolescence, but I never bothered to investigate. We were active in a culture that preached conversion therapy for gay men, and none of those rants about sinfulness applied to the Drew I knew—the Drew who played the piano for the Sunday service and sang solos in the weddings of all of our friends, the Drew who carried a Bible to class and never missed a church field trip or prayer meeting. In college, he took a real interest in science, and achieved multiple PhDs. But he stayed active in the church choir, avoiding at all costs the parties and fraternities and other low-hanging fruit of university life.

That night on the phone, as I registered what Drew was trying to tell me, my insides became very still. By the end of our call, I understood completely that I had never fully known my long-time friend, that there was so much more to him than he had ever given voice to, and that without any doubt in my mind, he had not, no matter what we had been told, chosen this.

The details of Drew's life are not mine to tell, though I feel compelled to let you know that shortly after our phone call, he came out to his loving and supportive parents, who cried but also said they'd been waiting their whole lives for that conversation. Today Drew lives happily as a scientist in New York City, finally being his truest self, continuing to regale his hundreds of friends with hilarious stories and enthusiastic dance moves. We have both come a long way from the days when we spent hours driving the back roads of Oklahoma, dreaming of a way out.

Drew's coming out marked a milestone for me as well, and he has given me permission to take this part of his story for myself. Because when we hung up the phone after his non-disclosure disclosure, I no longer believed things that I had believed just ninety minutes before. And if I didn't believe those things, what else did I not believe? Was my faith really so weak as to have been built upon the sand? Or does another human staring back at you transcend your desire to be "right," and instead invoke the compassion that should have been there all along?

It's been a long time now since that call, and it was harder for me then to separate out what I actually believed and knew to be true versus what various institutions had told me I should believe. I no longer buy into anything—from religion, to art, to feminism—hook, line, and sinker. For a while, this was disorienting—frustrating, even—after having thought so long in black and white. I had dabbled in shades of gray in my beliefs before, but Drew's revelation was a turning point. The comfort of believing that one interpretation, one political party, one philosophy held all the answers disappeared into the balmy Los Angeles smog. And that, too, was a freedom.

● ● ●

The day I met Jeff, I came home and told my roommate, "I met my new boss today. He looks homeless."

I wasn't exaggerating. When we were introduced, Jeff had thick, greasy hair down to his shoulders, which he covered in an old brown knit beanie. There was barely a chill in the air in December in LA, yet he had kept his heavy canvas coat on over a big, stained sweatshirt, dark jeans, and ratty shoes. He didn't rise from the chair as I poked my head around the door for an introduction, and he barely lifted a chin in greeting. I thought his aloofness was rude, but realized later that he was shy and focused, two traits that don't always make the best first impression.

Still, there was something about his presence. Soon after I had accepted a position as a production assistant on his first feature film for Paramount, I noticed how he quietly commanded a room. In his world, everything was in orbit around him. If someone made a joke, if someone landed a skate trick, if someone offered a thought or suggestion of any kind, everyone looked to Jeff for approval, which he gave or withheld in the subtlest of ways. There was no mistake who was in charge.

All of this was appealing. I was no stranger to powerful people in politics or religion, but Hollywood was new to me, and making art is different. This generous display of leadership was like nothing I'd ever seen.

When I met Jeff, I believed in a lot of absolutes. Morality was a battle between right and wrong. Actions were black or white. People were good or evil. No one had taught me about all the gray. I watched this man lead a merry band of fun in a subculture full of addiction and bad choices. I watched him encourage and forgive and employ all kinds of people. He loved his work, and he loved the people around him. He saw so much good in others and in the world, and he translated it onto the screen and behind the scenes. I'd never met anyone like him—so unaffected, so confident in who he was and what he was creating. I was in awe. I'm still in awe.

Working on *jackass the movie* with Jeff at the helm was a trip. I had never seen the popular TV show and was not at all familiar with the cast of characters or the skateboard magazine world from which they'd sprung in the late 1990s. In the beginning, I didn't find the cast or crew to be cute or charming; they seemed dirty and dangerous. I took the job because it was a major studio film, and I knew I was lucky to land a spot on the call sheet, no matter that I was the lowest person on the totem pole. The guys and their surrounding world were equally baffled by me. I was a bottle-blonde Oklahoma girl fresh from the sorority house who didn't cuss or do drugs or understand their jokes. We stared at one another like aliens from another planet. But their humor and camaraderie grew on me, and a few weeks in, I felt like part of a family, a small piece of something bigger and more important than me.

Through Jeff's eyes, I started to see everyone differently.

Every day I spent working on that movie, I loosened up a little more. I became less judgmental. After a long year of finishing college, going through a breakup and subsequent depression, and moving to Los Angeles and starting over, my heart started to heal and open. Working alongside the types of people I had been taught to judge, to steer clear of, to publicly pronounce myself separate from, and then to learn that they were, in fact, some of the most kind, generous, and accepting people I'd ever met, was my first lesson in broken people leading the way. Jeff showed me that in them.

My birthday that year fell at the end of the final shoot. I had been in Los Angeles just ten months. Jeff, as my boss and now my friend, put together a birthday dinner at an Italian place in the heart of Hollywood, not far from our production offices. I wore a blue halter top and wedge heels. Our large table was in a loft area above the rest of the restaurant, and they bought me a wildly inappropriate cake with a cartoon of my face on a cowgirl body. The dinner was loud and boisterous, as that was the only way this crew knew how to be.

Afterward, as we all stumbled outside in the dark toward Hollywood Boulevard, Jeff pulled out a wad of cash and handed it to the homeless man singing on the corner with a cap at his feet. He asked him to sing "Happy Birthday" to the pretty girl in the blue top, and what followed was the most beautiful melody I'd ever heard. There's a photo of me from this moment. I'm bent over at the waist, leaning forward toward the singer, Jeff and friends are in a semi-circle around us. My face is lit from within. There's a wine glow on my cheeks, but also something else. Something like gratitude. Something like joy. The delighted, unlined face of a girl who had spent her whole life scared but stood on that midnight street corner in a state of utter belonging.

All of these changes in me happened because of Jeff. If we'd never fallen in love, never gotten married, Jeff Tremaine would still belong in this chapter.

● ● ●

When I had been a mother for a little over three years, standing on a carousel in the park, I made a decision. It was a sunny day, too bright for me. I wore big sunglasses and still felt like the California sun was accosting me with its strength. The carousel music was loud in my ears, and the trees were whirring by, adding to the slight dizziness I had been fighting for weeks. One arm was holding up my son as he sat on the polyurethane horse, and my other hand was steadying my toddler daughter atop the zebra. Jeff stood behind us, a little to the left, whooping and cheering with each revolution of the carousel. I turned my face away from my family, out toward a parking lot in the distance and the mountains behind that. Tears started streaming down my face, unbidden. I couldn't have stopped them if I'd tried. But anyway, both hands were otherwise occupied.

If you had asked me why I was crying, I couldn't have told you. Things were going well, mostly. And yet I'd been crying off and on like this for months. When I wasn't crying, I was angry. I snapped at my babies and at Jeff. One day, I was picking up the living room and said out loud to the kids, "You guys, Mommy is so . . ." And my three-year-old daughter looked up and finished my sentence: "Tired." It had become a mantra, I guess.

Mommy is so tired.
Mommy is so tired.
Mommy is so tired.

I *was* tired, but it was more than that. I told myself that motherhood was tiring; my weariness wasn't something to raise any alarm bells on. I told myself maybe I just wasn't a baby person. I told myself it would pass. I told myself I was fine.

I told everyone else I was fine, too. My mom and sister had both expressed concern, but I had brushed them off. Jeff never did anything except believe me, so when I told him I just needed more sleep, that hormones were always wackadoo after children, that this was just how I felt now, it was life-after-kids Laura, he let it go. And I meant all of that when I said it. Never mind that my youngest was eighteen months old, well past the window of expecting things to "even out."

So on the carousel, as I was crying, the conclusion came to me so strongly it was almost audible:

I need help.

I need help.

I need help.

I'd never been to therapy before. Looking back, my first session with Kathleen was not a harbinger of what was to come. I sat in the corner of the couch, clinging to its velvet arm. In later years, I would place myself in the middle and arrange the throw pillows around me strategically. I didn't know how to tell Kathleen what was wrong because I didn't even *know* what was wrong. I bragged quite a bit, about Jeff, the kids, the readership of my online blog. I believe I told her I'd had an idyllic childhood and that none of my current issues stemmed from my parents or growing up. All my time in Oklahoma was pure perfection, I said, Norman Rockwell-esque. Anyway, I told her, my real life didn't even begin until I moved to LA at twenty-two. We could start there, maybe? To her credit, she kept a straight face.

At the end of that first session, Kathleen looked me straight in the eye and told me that I was hard to talk to. Before I could register surprise at such a statement—I was pretty sure I had chattered on charmingly for the full hour—she went on to explain that I talked over her, didn't let her get a word in edgewise, and she wasn't sure if it was going to work out, but we could give it another try the next week.

I was stunned and embarrassed by her assessment. My face grew red and hot with shame, but before she was even finished speaking, I knew that what she was saying was true. What made me want to die as I left the room, nodding through tears, fumbling for my car keys, was that the things she had told me weren't going to work in therapy were the things I prided myself on. Not the talking over her, but the crafted humble brags and occasional punch lines, and definitely the authority in my voice, the self-awareness and intelligence I thought I was displaying. These were things I thought were endearing about me. In an effort to make a good impression, I had pulled from the same bag of tricks I employ in any sort of social situation. That Kathleen saw right through it so quickly kicked me all the way off my personal pedestal.

Jeff was sprawled out on our bed when I got home from the session with Kathleen.

"Do I talk over you?" I asked, sniffling and curling into the comforter beside him. He laughed lightly, unsure how to answer. Was he supposed to be indignant on my behalf? Was he supposed to be honest in the interest of helping me work through my issues? He neither confirmed nor denied the statement in my question.

"It's true, what she said," I cried. "I know it's true."

That was the unsightly beginning, but the next session

was different. I let Kathleen ask questions. I let there be silence when I didn't know what to say instead of rushing to fill the space. I went religiously every week. I realized early on that many of my stated reasons for finally calling a therapist were not at all the reasons I needed to continue therapy. It is hard work to excavate your soul to get to the root truths that show up in your life and in your body as problems or patterns. A good therapist will help you scrutinize each new layer.

It is not hyperbole to say that working with Kathleen changed me. Therapy was not a wave-your-wand magic pill. I went on to have a terrible time full of panic attacks and despair in the months after I started therapy. Part of that was circumstantial and centered around a summer full of calamities, but also, healing yourself at the soul level hurts. If you're doing it right, you have to acknowledge you've been wrong sometimes, about yourself and others.

We started with my acute postpartum mental health issues and then we worked backward, untangling the stories I had told myself about my childhood and the untruths I had long believed about my worthiness and my role in relation-ships. Patterns emerged around my lifelong anxiety, and I was free in that room to say anything, no matter how selfish or damning or unkind or superstitious. Six years in, and I haven't managed to surprise Kathleen once.

Working with Kathleen changed me because I let it. Because I wanted to change. Not everything we seek works out, of course, but if it's change we're craving, there is change available to us. I could write reams about working with Kathleen and how it transformed my whole life. I am a huge therapy advocate. But the real fork in the road came that day on the carousel, when I stepped off that spinning wheel, and reached for help.

• • •

If therapy was the first step to coming back to myself after
marriage and babies, then Pilates was the second. Don't worry,
this is not a section about exercise. I will not extoll the virtues
of cardio. But I do want to share with you a little bit about
my physical body, however cringe-worthy that might be. This
story starts with a thirty-something-year-old woman unable
to complete a single sit-up.

I called and made my first Pilates appointment after a
friend raved about how the low-impact exercise was changing
her body. I trusted her review, and I desperately wanted to feel
and look better. This was the same friend who had a trampo-
line in her backyard. After the first bounce, I had to crawl off
the contraption in shame. Liquids had poured forth out of my
body with just one jump and subsequent landing. I laughed it
off as the unfortunate side effect of motherhood, but inside I
burned with embarrassment.

My bodily ailments were not unusual, but they were taking
up more and more of my life. The traumatic delivery of my daughter had left my lower internal organs out of place. I was battling
incontinence that was far worse than any cross-your-legs-when-
you-pee mom joke. After consulting with a urologist, I knew that
if I wanted to stave off surgery, I had to build up the muscles
of my destroyed pelvic floor. Pilates promised to do just that.

Starting Pilates was a master class in humiliation. I purposefully chose a studio full of real bodies and not full of hot
LA actresses, but it was still a huge ego hit when I couldn't do
anything my Pilates instructor, Kerri, was asking of me, and
they were very basic asks. Standing, I couldn't touch my toes.
Lying down, I couldn't lift my legs in the air. I couldn't sit up

from any position without help. I looked young, healthy, and slim on the outside. Pilates showed me that I was fooling myself and everyone else with this image. I had grown extraordinarily weak.

I can see now that there was a direct correlation between my mental health and my physical health. Sure, there are biological factors to both. And when you're young, you have more natural strength and more energy to hold it together when either falter. But I was aging, and regular life and motherhood had drained my ability to keep up the facade. In the years after motherhood, when my mental health spiraled, so did any strength in my body. I was able to ignore it because it happened slowly, while I was busy with other things.

Kerri was patient with me. When tears leaked down my face, and I bit my lower lip in shame, she explained gently that pain gets stored in the body. By moving myself in this way, I was releasing that pain, because the movement gives it permission to go. I heard her, but I didn't really understand. My mind was so disconnected from my body that they felt like two totally separate beings, and it was a long time before there was any real fusion between them. I decided early on to trust the process, much like I had done in therapy. The first time I sat up on my own in Pilates class, the entire studio burst into applause, and I burst into tears. There was a glimmer of something in that moment. The first tiny spark.

Pilates started to change my body and, more importantly, it changed my relationship to my body. Except to the trained eye, I don't really think I looked that different, but I held myself differently. I became acutely aware of how my body moved through the day. I cared about my posture. I paid attention to aches and pains and what they might be telling me. I noticed the strength it took when I carried a sleeping kiddo up the stairs to bed. I felt each muscle when I strained to retrieve something from an upper cabinet. I'm not sure I'd ever truly occupied my body before.

Something about the act of opening my body, physically broadening my shoulders, rooting myself to the ground when I walked—this cracked open something within me that I had been protecting for a long time. My spiritual heart opened. I gained a compassion that I had stuffed down when it didn't align with how I viewed the rest of the world. Previous to this, so many things were stymied by how closed off I had become to my own spirit and body. The writing I was doing online, my marriage and motherhood, all of those things had become muffled in the thrum of *get through the day, get through the day*. My mental health, my body, my work, and my relationships were all affected.

I made appointments for therapy and Pilates for valid, on-paper reasons. I thought I had postpartum depression and anxiety, and I for sure had pelvic floor issues. But working on those two pieces of the puzzle ended up being just the beginning of the big-picture healing of my heart and body.

Giving attention to my health and my past changed me and changed my future. As my heart opened and my body strengthened, I could feel myself getting back to my true core. It took work—and outside help—to scrub down the layers and find the true Laura. She'd always been waiting for me.

Your Turn

I want you to pretend your life has been a major motion picture, the opening credits rolling as you emerged from the womb screaming into the world, right up until today, the day you're reading this. What would be the major plot points? The plot twists? When did the "movie" change tone?

When my kids started elementary school, I made a new set of mom friends. These friendships developed fast, and it wasn't long before I realized that these women knew only a very specific slice of me. They knew the version of me who had landed before them, with a child in the same school with their child. They didn't know how I grew up or the choices I'd made to get myself here.

Each time a story from one of our pasts came up, it was like a revelation. "I didn't know that about you!" we'd exclaim. Because of course, we didn't. How could we? You can be pretty far into a friendship before you discover or reveal the moments that changed your future.

But this can be a rich and important conversation. What you're saying is, "I used to be something else, and now I'm this."

Like the stories I've included here, your moments of change may not have come when everyone expected it. All the more reason to talk about them.

Here are a few phrases to help you identify when it changed:

I divide my life as Before _____ and After _____.
I never looked at her/him/them/it the same way again.
I didn't realize how bad it was until it got better.
When I see that younger version of myself in photos,
 I just want to hug her.

Change has happened to you, whether you wanted it or not. If it was unwelcome, how do you feel about it now? If it's change you're currently seeking, you can share that too. Remember: change is always available to you.

Books That Shaped
My Worldview

(Listed in the order I read them.)

1. *Starring Sally J. Freedman as Herself* by Judy Blume
2. *It* by Stephen King
3. *The Screwtape Letters* by C. S. Lewis
4. *Franny and Zooey* by J. D. Salinger
5. *Frankenstein* by Mary Shelley
6. *Traveling Mercies* by Anne Lamott
7. *A Woman of Independent Means* by Elizabeth Forsythe Hailey
8. *Columbine* by Dave Cullen
9. *The Gifts of Imperfection* by Brené Brown
10. *The Body Keeps the Score* by Bessel van der Kolk

Chapter
EIGHT

What Broke You?

This is an essential question, but it is not one that should be asked early on in a friendship. Because while some people wear their brokenness on the outside, most of us are invested in shoving our hurt into the corners of our souls and not letting it leak out onto our pretty outfits. It's normal to acknowledge our brokenness, but not want to talk about it much. Why ruin a perfectly lovely afternoon with tears? And let's be honest. We don't always have a ton of patience for other people's broken places. One of the highest values our culture teaches is that we should pull ourselves up and keep marching. There is laundry to be done, and there are wars to wage. The other side of brokenness is part of the American Dream. We're not taught to get ahead by saying, "I was broken and . . . I'm still broken."

There's an attitude I've watched go down online and in person for a long time where people diminish their own brokenness in deference to another person's (worse) brokenness. It comes from a good place, a polite and thoughtful place. But the result is millions of people stuffing their cracks with coping mechanisms instead of experiencing true healing.

It's not that all circumstances are created equal. Of course *they're not. The death of a loved one isn't on par with a bad breakup. Losing your job isn't equal to the depths of despair found in natural disasters. So when we're faced with horrific circumstances in the world, we don't bring up our own grievances, because we're not stupid. We know they're not the same. One neglected childhood isn't the same as a Seriously Awful Situation.*

And yet it's hard to know ourselves and be known if we can't work through and talk about the things that really broke us. What makes it even more complicated is that we can't always articulate exactly why something was the final straw, or why it cut us to the core. Sometimes, the thing that caused us the most grief doesn't look all that bad from the outside. Maybe it just doesn't seem clear why it left a fracture. It can be complicated to explain.

Recently, a friend was telling me about an intense argument with her spouse, a terrible fight that culminated in a discussion about divorce. As she was explaining the circumstances to me, I felt baffled about why it led them to start talking about splitting up. The fight was kind of about money. And even though I could see it went deeper than that, I would have had to know layers upon layers of backstory and innuendo and, of course, a third party can't always know all that. So I heard what she was saying, but I didn't totally understand it.

But that's okay, because that's how it is with brokenness. Aside from events that are clear traumas, the things that break us might be the result of actions that built up over time. They might seem petty or immature or make you out to be a fragile person. So let's just start by agreeing that no one else gets to tell you that your broken places aren't valid. You know in the deepest part of your soul what broke and why.

I'll Go First

In the early spring of my fourth-grade year, my little group of girlfriends and I met at the YMCA to celebrate the end of a successful basketball season with an after-school swim. We were not basketball players; we were cheerleaders, a DIY group of ten-year-olds who bought blue and gold sweat suits from Walmart and ironed on spirit decals in a varsity font. One of the moms had volunteered to teach us a few cheers, and we showed up every Saturday to cheer at the rec league games, played by our male classmates. The 1980s was, of course, a different time in parenting. Kids had more spontaneity and a longer leash. Parents dropped us off at public places for hours at a time and expected us to be there when they came back, whenever that was.

So on this Friday afternoon, our gaggle of giggly girls stumbled out of the locker room alone, five or six of us in brightly colored one-pieces, tiptoeing across the cold tile to the empty pool area.

Only it wasn't exactly empty. At the far end of the Olympic-sized pool stood a boy about our age, staring down in the water. He had on red swim trunks, bright against his dark skin. He was silent and still.

Most of the girls in this friend group were familiar with the Y. Swim classes and birthday parties were common at the pool, with its thick, plastic, primary-colored lane dividers floating in the water, cheers and shrieks magnified by the fully turquoise-tiled room, a soft blue tint on everything owing to the few windows. So it was a little eerie for the space to be so big and so quiet, and when our first laugh echoed off the walls, we slapped our hands over our mouths and stifled our own reactions to the cool water as we climbed in, one by one, using the metal ladder.

About half the group had entered the pool when the boy down at the far end hollered—or rather just spoke, but it seemed loud—that his friend was under the water. "What?" we shouted back, our splashing and chattering keeping his voice from being fully heard.

"My friend," he said, and pointed down into the deep end. "He's been down there a long time."

We could see a figure immersed in the water, who appeared to be sitting at the bottom of the pool. There were only a few beats of time between our comprehension of this and what happened next, but it felt like someone had pressed pause. We were ten years old, in the shallow end of the pool, staring across the expanse to the deep end. It took two slow blinks of an eye for heart-pounding recognition to set in.

Thinking much more quickly than I did, one of my friends climbed out and flung open the door to the pool area, in search of her teenage brother who was working out in the weight room across the hall. Dripping wet and scared, a few of us ran to the front desk where, for the first precious seconds, no one believed the hysterical children screaming that there was a boy in the bottom of the pool. Then, in slight disbelief and confusion, someone called an ambulance.

We were frantic in our return to the pool area, arriving just as an adult exited the men's locker room, barefoot and wearing a swimsuit. In seconds, the man assessed the situation and jumped in the water. Then there was yelling. I do not know where that sound was coming from or how long it lasted.

The next few minutes happened fast, and yet thirty years later, I still remember so much of it. The man pulled the boy up from the bottom of the pool and supported him with one arm while using his other to cling to the side. Another adult arrived and helped him haul the boy out of the water. They were performing CPR, and watery yellow vomit spilled down the boy's cheeks.

My friends and I stayed huddled in the corner, shivering, not speaking.

After the medics arrived, while they attended to the boy lying immobile in a puddle of pool water and bodily fluids, someone noticed our presence and escorted us off the scene. By then we had realized that the child pulled from the water was also our age, like his friend. By then we had recognized, yet not spoken of, the reality we'd witnessed.

We pulled on our makeshift cheerleading sweats without properly drying off, the cotton sticking to our bodies, still damp with the over-chlorinated water. The teenager who had run for help earlier piled us all into the back of his pickup truck. He drove our group to my house because I was the only latchkey kid among us.

We took turns calling our parents, telling them one by one that something had happened, and they should come right away. My own mom came home early, even though I hadn't been able to reach her when I called her at work. It was a small town, and word had traveled fast. It turned out that the boy's mother worked with my mom, and the police showed up and made an announcement to the staff. For a brief moment, before anyone identified the boy, my mom, who had known we were swimming at the Y that afternoon, had panicked.

She saw to it that each girl got home okay, and then she turned to me. We stood in the downstairs bathroom, shaky.

"He's going to be okay, though, right, Mom?" I pleaded.

"I mean, that was scary, but he'll be fine, right? Those people saved him?" I had turned things around in my head in the space of half an hour and had decided it was a happy ending, because anything else was too big to bear.

Mom was quiet for a few minutes. She looked at the sink, and then she looked back at me.

"No, Laura," she said softly. "No. He's not okay."

The boy had drowned in the pool before our eyes, yet I don't recall anyone talking with me about what I'd witnessed and how I felt about it. There were no crisis counselors. When the story was in the news, when there was a memorial service, I was never privy to any of those details. I didn't go to the Y—where I had previously been a regular—for a long, long time after that. Someone told me they changed their rules about swimming at your own risk.

My fourth-grade friends and I were silent about this thing that happened. We never tried to make sense of it by talking it through. I don't remember it coming up again for years, not until that same group of little girls had become young women in high school. We were no longer close, but our shared history kept us bonded. In a moment of vulnerability, the drowning we had witnessed came up between me and one of the girls, and we cracked wide open, right there on the sidewalk outside the sprawling brick cafeteria.

Yes, we cried. That event had broken us a little bit. It had changed our childhoods. Why weren't we ever encouraged to talk about it? No one had told us what to think about it. No one had guided any of us through the devastating revelation that some-one our own age could just die. It could have been any one of us. We knew this now, because we'd seen it. The boy's friend couldn't help. The adults couldn't save him. Our innocence was gone.

I am forty years old now, and I still think of that child and his family every single year in March, on the anniversary of the day they lost their son, their brother, their cousin. I am hyper vigilant around water. I don't like pools. It was a singular event that quietly affected so many, for so long.

●　●　●

In high school I belonged, by choice, to a sweet little non-denominational church out on the edge of town. I started attending with a friend whose dad was the preacher, after trying out denominations around town with other friends. Nothing felt right until I walked into Cross of Christ. The church was humble and dignified, and the sermons were smart and thoughtful. It didn't have the pomp and circumstance of other denominations; it wasn't showy or gimmicky. Nothing was dumbed down. I liked that. But best of all, there were thirty minutes of music at the beginning of the service—this was before the practice was common on Sunday mornings— and I was drawn in to all that singing. It was strange and wonderful to see adults being so vulnerable, often raising their hands in the air in worship or kneeling in holy supplication. It made my whole week better to stand and sing such beautiful songs collectively, in an air of prayer. This church and its people were truly sacred.

One Friday evening, as a special treat for our tiny, ten-person youth group, an out-of-town guest was brought in to speak to us. Kandi had the gift of prophecy, we were told, and she had a few words for the youth in our congregation.

In terms of the gifts of the Spirit, I went along with what was taught from the church's pulpit then: that we had no reason to believe any of the spiritual gifts laid out in the

Bible had fallen away. If you were blessed with the gift of tongues or prophesy, you were expected to heed that call. It was also understood that the gifts were not for everyone, and should you not possess one of the ancient gifts, or if you did not desire them enough to pray for such a burden to be bestowed upon you, then you were to support others as they lived out their calling.

Since my parents weren't churchgoers, nor did they know what was going on inside this small Bible church, I never felt the obligation to deny or encourage the increasingly overt displays of Christ followers at the special services. Hearing someone speak in tongues freaked me out, but I wanted to be supportive, so I mostly stayed quiet. Prophecy, on the other hand—well, that was exciting if it was personal. Who didn't want to know the future? I read my horoscope in the back of the teen magazines with glee, and this felt like it would be even better. This wasn't deciphered from the stars; this was a message straight from GOD. Right out of a pretty mouth.

Because Prophet Kandi was pretty. She looked like a Barbie doll—skinny and tall with big, blonde hair. As far as I was concerned, she had won the life lottery: young, beautiful, and trusted enough by our church elders to give a message to the body. I sensed right away that this was going to be a real event.

The special service was private, for the youth group only. There was a sermon, of sorts, from our youth pastor, and then a few general words from Kandi. And then we were encouraged to kneel on the carpeted stairs at the front, facing the baptismal, and remain in a prayerful pose as a prophecy was spoken over each of us.

I prayed fervently, but I also peeked between my arms

as they kept me balanced in position. Soft music played. Past my scrawny elbow, I watched as Kandi whispered her visions to each teenager in the room. There was Brittany, who drove in from the high school west of town, who pulled her hair down from its scrunchie to hide her face as she openly wept in response to whatever Kandi was saying to her. There was Carla, a homeschooled girl who was quick with a smile and was never afforded the grace she deserved by the public school kids.

Clint was the only boy active in the youth group and the only boy there that night. Kandi took an extra long time with him. I couldn't make out her words, but her tone was forceful and confident. She gestured, with one hand slicing into the other, making her points clear and direct. Clint's face was hidden in his praying arms, but I knew him well, and I imagined what he must have been feeling hearing this prophet's words over him, surely outlining his path of leadership. I knew he was feeling justified and humbled with the weight of the future. He would carry it like a shield of armor later, knowing what he had to do, and knowing he would emerge victorious. This is who he was, and Kandi was surely confirming that in his ear, just in front of the baptismal.

When Kandi was done speaking to Clint, who was kneeling a few feet to my right, she stood and brushed her long, blonde hair out of her face. She told the group to rise and murmured that she was going to close our time together in prayer.

But wait! I wanted to cry out. *She skipped me!* I tried to catch the eye of the youth pastor's wife, thinking she would speak up for me. While Kandi gave her benediction, my thoughts raced from the pain of being rejected, to the injustice of being the only one without a prophecy, to the deep fear that she had seen my future and it was too bleak to outline in this holy room. Perhaps Kandi had seen that I would be dying in very short order, and she was going to spare me that advance knowledge.

The prayer ended and people started hugging, their faces red and puffy from emotion and dehydration. I stood up from the floor, disoriented and crushed. Still, no one would make eye contact with me. It would be at least another decade before my faith fully unraveled, but that night I became a skeptic. I didn't think Kandi was a scam artist, but I sensed that she had indeed seen the path God had paved for me, and she had chosen not to share it.

It felt like she was withholding information that didn't suit her. I was the only kid there that she didn't speak to or look at, the only one without parents in the church. I was constantly looking for spiritual guidance and felt constantly lost and alone. If even God—via prophet Kandi—didn't have words for me, then what was I doing here? Why was I trying so hard to make my faith stick?

Meanwhile, the other youth group members seemed so moved by whatever words Kandi had spoken to them that I couldn't bear to unload my packed emotions about being the sole attendee without a prophecy and my suspicion that it wasn't an accident. I haven't shared this Prophet Kandi story very often. For many years, it was too tender. I was embarrassed, and when I thought about it, I would get mad all over again. Only now can I see that this story isn't about knowing the future; it's about being skipped over. It's about being left out when others are chosen. It's about feeling worthy, until something subtly says you're not.

I have felt alone for most of my faith journey. I came to

Jesus at a camp a thousand miles away from my parents; I attended church on my own for all of my childhood; I left the church without anyone begging me to stay. It's not supposed to be this way. Religion is supposed to give us earthly words and rituals and community to be in communication with the spiritual realm. I had no guidance, no anchor, no one telling me where to go, what to read, or who to believe. Or rather, there was an abundance of information on all of these things, but they were confusing and contradictory for a child. Even as an adult, after all of this, I still struggle to make sense of it.

I stayed active in that wonderful church for years after that night when Prophet Kandi skipped me. But when my faithfulness broke years later, and I traced back all the cracks in the road, I knew that the special service that night was the first time I consciously thought, *I don't know if I believe this anymore.*

Not the part about God, but the part about being chosen. Being saved. Being left behind. Those ideas fractured when I stood up from prayer, with my carpet-burned knees, angry and determined. And broken.

●   ●   ●

I lost my virginity deliberately to a boy I loved. I was twenty-one years old.

I did not, in the weeks immediately following, feel like a bad person. I was thrilled by the meaningful connection and, honestly, a bit relieved not to wait anymore. I'd been saving myself for marriage for so long that once I realized I didn't want to get married anytime soon, the waiting seemed less crucial. I don't know when that flip switched in my mind.

The tenor of that vow changed as my twenties stretched

before me. I don't want to portray that my first time was a non-event, because it was a very, very big event in my heart. But in the moments following, my thoughts were along the lines of, *This is it? This is the thing that we orient our entire lives around? This bodily function has brought down monarchies?*

Before I convinced this poor boy to wear the mantle of my virginity for the rest of our lives, I had let the whole world know about my purity. I preached it. I wore the symbolic ring. No matter that I'd come right up to the line time and time again over years of dating, my hymen remained intact, and therefore, so did my soul. Jesus didn't dwell in the details, I decided.

And then, well. Then. This is awkward to write about. It doesn't make a ton of sense even all these years later. So I'll try to say it plainly: my body rebelled. Not long after I started having sex, my nether regions developed an emergency medical issue that was painful and embarrassing. I don't want to go into details here because we're talking about my genitals, so I will just say that it was not an STD or pregnancy. The problem was my body—a malfunction, a defect. And I believed in my heart of hearts that it was God's punishment for giving away my virginity before marriage.

Now listen, this wasn't theology I had ever been taught. The church I grew up attending was not fire and brimstone; it did not preach the mathematics of divine punishment (which had been explained to me in detail when I visited the Baptist youth group). And yet in my deepest soul, I believed that this conclusion was obvious. I had gone against what I knew was right, and now the punishment fit the crime.

I explained as much to the doctor. Through wracking sobs in the examination room, I told her the timeline between my first forays into sexuality to my leap into penetration, and now this—this awful, painful affliction affecting my vagina. I read in her concerned face first confusion and then pity and then, briefly, fury.

"That's not how God works," she stated flatly. "If that were how God worked, this practice would be overrun with patients." She was not the type of doctor to delve further into my emotional feelings about my medical problem, but I sensed she had a thousand words she could have spewed in response to my lost-virginity-punishment logic.

My whole life I have balanced right on the edge between a fierce rational side and a tendency toward all things spiritual. This sex-now-surgery converged every single part of that. I couldn't shake what I felt on the intuitive side, but I couldn't rationalize it, either. The thing that broke my spirit was not the act in the bed, nor the physical trauma that followed. What took me down for a long, long time after this was that I believed God had seen me, and that he was angry and disappointed, so much so that he unleashed his power on my vagina. I felt seen by the Creator of the universe, and what he saw was displeasing.

I felt very alone as I was breaking down, not just because the nature of the subject made it taboo to discuss, but also because I looked around for secret signs that anyone else was having a similar existential and physical dilemma. Of course, I had friends who were sexually active, and of course, I had friends who had mixed feelings about all kinds of sexually-related things or even just regular life things. But no one else seemed to be battling a lightning strike from the Lord himself. Most of my peers' sexual angst was theoretical, and yet here I was with a biological, somewhat crippling condition that appeared to be a direct result of my choices.

If asked outright, I would have adamantly argued that this was NOT how the God of the universe operated. Except now that it was happening to me, I *did* believe it. After multiple exhausting, debilitating, and emotionally draining medical procedures, it was a surgery that cured me. But I have to tell you that I carried that broken piece of myself for a very long time. It took years and years and years to untangle all of my feelings about sex and God and our own bodies punishing us. As soon as I thought I was past it, the pain—physically and emotionally—returned: when I delivered my children; when, once again, everything below my waist didn't cooperate. It was a wound to my body and my psyche that ran very, very deep.

Brokenness is like that. You may think you've healed a particular wound, but then it shows up again when you least expect it. It challenges everything you worked so hard to stitch back together. We want to believe that the areas where we were broken scar stronger than before, but in my experience, those lines stay tender. You have to take care—as much as you can—not to test it too hard.

The whole situation did a real number on a young person convinced that everything is connected, and nothing is an accident. I had a few years when I tried to believe it was all an unrelated accident of biology, nothing to see here, everything-turned-out-fine-so-let's-not-dwell-on-it, but that wasn't exactly right, either.

Here's what I believe about it now. My body had an internal defect at birth. Sex exacerbated this condition, which was easily fixable with a small surgery. Those are the facts, and they are irrefutable. If I could go back and sit down with twenty-something-year-old Laura, I would take her hand and explain carefully that the medical problems that followed the loss of her virginity were not her fault. They were not a message from God. Twenty-something Laura would not believe forty-something Laura, but she might be glad to see brokenness has a beautiful future.

●　　●　　●

In the summer of 2012, I accepted an invitation to travel to Sri Lanka with a group of other writers and bloggers in order to highlight the work a popular nonprofit was doing on that side of the world. I was hesitant to step that far out of my comfort zone. I wasn't yet aware of the legitimate criticisms of poverty tourism, but I had the platform to spread some good in the world. So it seemed appropriate to squelch my own fears if the objective was to bring relief and awareness to a part of the world that didn't get much press. It was an easy yes for me, though not without complications.

On the trip were seven other bloggers, only two of whom I knew. Our flights converged in New York City, and then we all flew through the night to Dubai before the final leg to Sri Lanka. At the airport, I greeted the women I knew, and I shook hands with a shy man in a bow tie, another friendly face with a goatee, and nodded politely at the bald guy in the corner who only briefly glanced up from his phone.

To put it mildly, we all had strong personalities. We all came in with our ingrained belief systems and the ability to land a strong point. I wasn't the only person who had mixed feelings about being on the trip, so our united skepticism hung in the air, hoping to be proven wrong.

Within hours of landing in Sri Lanka, we accidentally stumbled onto a ceremony happening in the small village we were visiting. Jet-lagged and in culture shock, the group of us held hands so as not to get separated among the pressing crowds. As if a group of startled white people would be hard to find in rural Sri Lanka.

Most of the ceremony revolved around a fire walking ritual, during which men, clothed only in brightly colored loin cloths, ran across burning coals as a faith exercise in purification. There was a pounding drum and the sounds of whoops and cheers as the men, sometimes solo, sometimes two or more at a time, ran across the strip of smoldering fire.

On the outskirts of the fire walk, but still very much within the crowd, large bulls wandered through, people ducking and dodging their large horns.

It was a special thing we were witnessing, but it was also frightening. The sights and smells were overwhelming. The shouting in a language we didn't understand meant we couldn't tell if we were in danger, if we were supposed to join in, or if our very presence was offensive.

The latter might have been true, but no one stopped us from observing. The Sri Lankan adults pointedly ignored us while the children peeked out from under skirts to stare at our pale skin and foreign clothes. Our local guides seemed equal parts excited to show off their customs and also a little agitated that we were there at all.

I thought of my tiny American babies at home, with their drawers full of clothes and abundance of food and drink, playing with newly purchased toys in a temperature-controlled home. It seemed unfair, suddenly—all of it. I closed my eyes tight against a wave of homesickness.

I hadn't prepared my heart or mind adequately for Sri Lanka. Over the course of the week, I was stunned by the poverty. It is one thing to know about a place or a condition intellectually, and it is another to witness it firsthand. It broke my spirit to see the contrast between the resources and basic needs of Sri Lanka and the United States. I had spouted a lot of opinions theoretically for a long time, about politics and religion and bootstraps and aid. It's easy to talk about who deserves help and personal accountability from the comfort of a first world home. But all philosophical arguments are lost when you're faced with a human in need in front of you. I'm embarrassed that I have to keep learning this.

We spent our time in Sri Lanka traveling between villages, seeing with our own eyes the contrast between the places where the charity had been rooted for years with American aid and the struggling communities for whom help was still on the way. These villages were often hundreds of miles apart from one another, so we spent hours and hours in the passenger van—sometimes up to eight hours a day—between the sites we were visiting and the hotel that was our home base.

During these van rides, with no cell phone service and no other distractions, the eight of us had nothing to do but talk. The first day or so, chatting came easily. We told our backstories and shared about our current work online or in publishing. We spoke animatedly about the presidential election happening back home. We went through the best movies or TV shows we'd seen lately. It was surreal to climb out of the van after these conversations and spend lunchtime in the midst of some of the most abject poverty we'd ever encountered. Many of the Sri Lankan people we were visiting were suffering. They had to walk miles for water every day, and disease was pervasive. We were weary and chagrined filing back into the air-conditioned vehicle, and there started to be stretches of silence.

It was around day three when someone openly broke. I don't remember who was first, but we all toppled, one by one. The shiny overviews of our lives that we'd shared on day one were washed away as details came spilling forth about mental illness and toxic marriages, losing a child, an abusive parent. Our strong professional veneers cracked as we rode along the dusty Sri Lankan roads.

Once you are broken open, once your wounds are laid bare for all to see, there are no take backs. Individually and collectively, we were seeing our own scars in the light of this global disparity, and it changed the shape of them. We started to release the petty hurts we'd been clinging to, and we started to confront the bigger-picture mistakes and traumas we were living with. Our world back home felt like a fantasy. Sri Lanka felt like the truth.

You cannot unknow what you now know. The wondrous faces, expressing both joy and need, in that beautiful country changed how I looked at my own life and money and aid and foreign policy. So many systems are so broken. So much is unfair. Much is required of us.

And the people who took that journey with me, well, we were broken together. Our lives back in the States differed greatly, but we cycled together through the emotions of gratitude and understanding. There was something that happened in that van, among tears and sweat and knowledge that will stay with me for the rest of my life. It was our own inadvertent version of the cleansing of the sacred fire walking ritual.

I came home from Sri Lanka broken, and my mental health continued to collapse over the next year. It was an incredibly sad and stressful season, blurry and full of grief, and I spent many days on autopilot just to get through them.

My children were so young that they could have been a healthy distraction from the hardships of the world except that Finch, a happy, sweet baby, had started waking throughout the night. I hadn't yet connected my lack of sleep and panic attacks, but for over a year, my mind didn't work right. I didn't call the pediatrician, ask for outside help, or in any way try to fix all of the things that were wrong. I was in pure survival mode.

The panic attacks came so frequently that they dulled into one long wave of anxiety I rode all the time. My hands shook. I was weepy and short of breath. I snapped at people and got defensive when my mom, sister, and close friends gently suggested that I wasn't doing so well. When I look back at pictures from the years when Finch was a toddler, I see a lot of emptiness in my eyes.

Still, we muddled through. I kept writing and writing and writing. Jeff made another hit movie. After a year or so, Finch started sleeping again. I went to therapy and did the hard work. And then we faced back-to-back crises in our extended family. Our niece was hospitalized for twelve weeks. Another niece, just six years old, fell into a coma following a history of seizures. We lost loved ones tragically and suddenly. All of this left us gutted and hollow. We were broken.

I look back on these years now, and in some ways, it feels like it was someone else living them. As in, I remember my childhood and twenties clearly, and the last few years of my thirties remain sharp and Technicolor. But for a handful of years, from 2012–2015, it's all a little foggy. I wasn't myself. I want to shelve that time with grace, and sharing about it now will help me to stay rooted and present when faced with the next dark season. Even as broken places heal, things are never quite the same as they were before.

Your Turn

What broke you?

This is the hardest question in the book. I know that our souls are sensitive to the things that break us, and those things are often tender to talk about. I want to reiterate that you should be careful whom you trust with your secrets. Your pain probably has layers to it, and whether your story is especially remarkable or somewhat mundane, we're talking about your hurt here. The ultimate "stuff" in sharing your stuff.

I don't write this chapter or this advice lightly. It might be best to sit with your journal first and work through the things that most matter to your past and your present in terms of brokenness. If it feels right, take this pain to therapy. I'm a huge advocate for therapy; I think it's for anyone and everyone, and it might be helpful to process these soft parts of your story with a professional before you offer them to the world at large.

A few thoughts on sharing your broken stuff:

1. **Maybe don't blurt it out at a table full of giddy girls-night-out-goers.** Or at a group playdate with toddlers underfoot. Don't put yourself in a position to be disappointed by another person's reaction because they're in the wrong mood or distractions abound. They won't be able to give your story the attention it needs, and you will leave the interaction feeling like they didn't care or didn't "get it." Timing is everything when you're entering into a conversation about brokenness.

2. **You get to choose what matters to you.** Do not feel obligated to put your brokenness into a "big picture" context. You do not have to be objective when you're talking

about being broken. If it's not immediately obvious, you might give a little backstory or explanation for why something affected you the way it did, but it is not your job to convey your trauma in the most generous way toward others. The friend listening can fill in her own blanks about what is not being said.

3. **Be a good listener when someone is sharing their stories of brokenness with you.** I know we try to empathize by volleying back our own hard, similar stories, but read the room on whether that's appropriate or not. It's probably not.

4. **Be gentle with yourself after you've shared.** Vulnerability hangovers are real (ask me how I know), and the day after you've shared something, it can feel like all the lights in the world are too bright. Give yourself grace in the hours or days following a hard conversation. Have a good cry, go to bed early, be grateful for the gift of time.

Sharing your most broken places isn't easy, but it pulls the darkest parts toward the light when you tell someone about your scars and soft spots. You can't make sense of it, and you can't move forward when you simply hold onto it with your own hands. Healing happens when you let yourself be seen.

10 *Letters I Never Sent*

1. Dear Sweet Mary,

   There was never a more loving babysitter in all the world. You tapped into the very softest part of my soul and let it stay tender. Thank you for letting me stay the night when I "ran away from home." Thank you for sewing a quilt when I was a child to be given to me when I got married, and thank you for adding my mother's lace to my veil for my wedding day. So many of the gentle tendencies I have with my own children were learned on your lap.

2. Dear Mrs. Graham,

   You were a good teacher to me, even when I was a belligerent teenager, and it meant so much that you trusted me to be the middle school yearbook editor. I'm sorry I screwed it up so badly. I'm also sorry I told you Bill Clinton couldn't possibly win the presidency.

3. Dear Lauren M.,

   You were my first best friend and one of the smartest people I've ever met. I wanted to be like you for years, even after we drifted apart. I wish I knew what your life looks like now, but I hope it's everything you ever wanted.

4. Dear Mr. Stephen King,

   Maybe I'm not in your typical demographic. And I don't know or care if you met the devil at the crossroads all those years ago. I think you're the greatest storyteller alive. I can't wait until students are studying your work, right along with Shakespeare.

5. Dear Coach S.

Look, I know I wasn't a good enough performer to deserve the front position of that pyramid in drill team competition. The judges' scores reflected my terrible toe touch. You know it. I know it. But you are such a woman of integrity that you didn't crush my spirit or pull me from that lineup. Thanks?

6. Dear Dr. Bell,

It's funny to think back on our time as roommates during that first year in LA. Turns out you changed my life more than I could have imagined. Without your willingness to take a gap year before med school, without your connections to get us peon jobs at MTV, without your decency to look the other way while I awkwardly floundered around trying to find myself, I wouldn't be writing anything in this book. I'll never forget what we shared and what it meant.

7. Dear Bruce,

I know, I can't believe I remember your name, either. You took pity on a nervous girl stranded on the side of the road in Malibu with a flat tire outside cell phone service range. It is SO GREAT that you weren't a serial killer. And that you fixed my tire before one had the chance to idle by.

8. Dear T. the Wedding Planner,

It was unfair that you accused my bridesmaids of doing cocaine in the bathroom. None of us had ever done a single drug in our lives! (I think. Don't quote me on that.) Did you think that was happening because we came from Hollywood? You did do a great job dealing with the police when my brother-in-law punched a hole in the wall at the museum reception, though. That's what matters.

9. Dear Lady at the Airport,

You could have just walked by the familiar sight of a frazzled woman juggling a baby, a toddler, a stroller, and three bags. But you didn't. You stopped. You corralled us into a corner and helped me get reorganized. You offered kind words and a non-pitying smile. I think of you every time I spot another woman trying to handle it all, to help or just for an eye-lock of solidarity. You paid it forward, sister, and now I do my part to fill those shoes.

10. Dear Noah,

I honestly can't remember which of us created the email game GO, but it sustained me through a long season of working on a terrible TV show. The questions that we volleyed back and forth (GO!) that resulted in long, deep, navel-gazing emails had the makings of a real rom-com, but alas, we were both hopelessly in love with other people. It meant a lot, though, learning to ask and listen from behind a screen. As they say, the rest is history . . .

Chapter
NINE

Where Are Your Magical Moments?

Some moments in our lives are unexplainable. They have a little bit of glitter on them, a little bit of the supernatural. Sometimes the magic shows up as an omen or sign; sometimes something impossible happens or someone knows something they couldn't have possibly known, and yet they do. The more logical among us might try to reason these things away, but deep down, we know it when there is something special about an interaction or an event.

I collect these types of stories, even those that didn't happen to me. I love to hear someone tell how they were in the exact right place at the exact right time for some crazy thing to happen. I am fascinated by recountings that appear to be communiques from the spiritual realm. I've picked a few of my own magical moments to share here, all of them sacred to me.

Even though it's in my nature, I'm not going to live in a place of fear about what others will think after I've released these stories into the wild. This whole book is about sharing our stuff. I would never advocate that we tell our stories haphazardly, but we have to be in a place of trust with one another.

We are going to honor and not belittle one another's stories. The telling of them doesn't diminish their truth. The telling of them doesn't diminish their magic. I'm not going to share every single thing, nor are you.

But there is magic in the sharing, and there are stories in this magic.

I'll Go First

The first time I knew exactly what I was meant to do for the rest of my life—as clearly as if God himself had spoken an audible word into my ear—was on a mundane afternoon in eighth grade. It was hours after the final bell had rung, and the middle school was empty and quiet. I was barefoot in the English classroom, a large space by any standards, with fifteen-foot ceilings, on the top floor of the stately government building. The classroom doubled as the yearbook headquarters, and I was the yearbook editor. In the corner of the room was a converted closet functioning as a photography darkroom. That darkroom had a history of shenanigans. It doesn't have anything to do with this magical memory, but as I set the stage for the moment I'm about to tell you, the prominence of that corner closet comes to mind. Teenagers are sneaky—and naughty.

The room was empty save for me and one other classmate, a girl I'd known for years named Jill. I was small, a late bloomer, and still comfortable in my body. The other girls in my grade were turning into women, both inside and out, but I was still slight and underdeveloped. My feet were bare, this I remember. I must have kicked off my preppy loafers into the corner.

And I was standing, inexplicably, on top of the desks. They were lined up in a row, edge to edge, stretching from the chalkboard to the back wall, ultimately making a large U-shape around the room. During the school day, Mrs. Graham would stand in the middle and lecture about the text we were studying. That semester, we were doing a deep dive into *The Odyssey*. I was internalizing the hero's journey and the call of the Sirens. It was unlike anything I'd ever read before. I struggled with the text, honestly, and I avoided the deeper meaning behind the stories, just like I avoided thinking too hard about the dinosaurs. If I learned too much, I asked too many questions I didn't want to know the answers to. Where were the Greek gods and the tyrannosaurus on the earth's timeline? Did their existence come before or after the Bible? I dodged anything that put my faith on shaky ground.

Standing on top of these desks, the faux wooden veneer cool to my bony feet, I paced up and down the row. I was telling Jill a story, and I made it up as I went along. It was myth-like, the tale I was trying to weave. I think I was going for a spiritual explanation for why it rained. Or snowed? The main character was named Lexus. He wept over something, as I recall.

Jill sat sideways in one of the desks closer to the classroom door and listened politely. She picked at her long nails, glancing up periodically when my pacing stopped. I would occasionally plant my feet firmly on the desks in a stance that said I was making an important point. My storytelling was stream-of-consciousness and free-flowing. I gesticulated wildly, and my tone rose and fell. I started a tangent and then backtracked, already self-editing but in a good way and not an overly critical one.

At my invented myth's conclusion, I was breathless, full of joy. Jill clapped and giggled at my theatrics. But I felt it: there was magic in the air. Late afternoon light streamed warmly into the classroom, and I climbed down to earth a different person.

I have spent decades chasing that first feeling of flow. I thought for a long time that it was in the narrative details, in the actual fiction itself. I've written hundreds of thousands of words since then, in story form and otherwise, trying to get the tone and sentence just right. I love words on a page. But it didn't occur to me until right this very second, as I'm telling you this story, that as much as it was the creativity that was flowing out of my mouth, maybe I missed what was so special about that magical moment. Maybe, all along, it was the speaking. Using my literal voice, putting the words into the room to an audience of one. It wasn't the story, and it wasn't the words. It was the voice. My voice. Telling something. And all these years later, telling you.

• • •

My brother, Lance, deployed to Iraq as an officer in the Marine Corps in 2006. He was in danger every single day, though he lied to us about that in order to keep my parents sane. On the evening he told me he was being called up, I had a green cucumber face mask on and was wrapped in a robe. I sat on the edge of the bed and cried, but held the phone out from my gooey face, keeping my voice strong so he couldn't tell I was in the middle of a beauty ritual while he delivered this news, or that I was devastated by it.

At the time, Jeff and I had been dating for a couple of years. Lance departing for the Middle East brought some clarity into my life. I wanted a family. I wanted children. And I wanted them with Jeff. I believed we were made for one another, but Jeff was dragging his feet. An inkling had started to form in the back of my skull. I could move back to Oklahoma. I could help my brother run a new business. He would come home, I knew he would. It would be a life that made sense. Living in LA for a few years would turn out to be a fun detour in my journey, the kind of thing you tell your grandkids about wistfully.

That summer, after Lance left, I made a pact with one of my best friends, Lindsay, who was also dating an older guy hesitant on making forever vows. Lindsay and I had big dreams for ourselves and knew we shouldn't have to beg a man for them. We made a deal that we would not mention marriage or a future again before the new year. Not one time. And we were to tell no one. It wasn't an ultimatum with anyone except ourselves. It was a promise to one another. If, by the beginning of the new year, we were in the same place in our relationships, we would end them and move on. It was July.

Lindsay's boyfriend proposed on Halloween.

As the holidays approached, I could feel myself pulling away from Jeff and from my life in LA. A part of me was preparing to pack it all up. Thanksgiving came and went, and then one night, Jeff, over sushi and out of the blue, suggested we look for rings. I kept my face neutral. My body did not match what he seemed to be saying. He tossed the ring shopping out casually and I caught it equally nonchalantly. Part of me didn't believe it. We'd spent the holidays with my family in Oklahoma, but I had retreated so far back into myself that there was a growing distance between us.

And then, nothing happened. Jeff didn't bring up rings

again. I was sad as we kissed at midnight into the shiny new 2007. New Year's Eve was my deadline, and it felt like the fates had spoken. No answer is an answer.

Just a few days into January, my cell phone rang in the middle of the night. My brother was months into his deployment, but I still wasn't used to that shrill sound in the dark. The calls were always Lance, from the other side of the world, but in the few moments before I saw the caller ID, there loomed the terrible possibility that someone else would be on the line with heartbreaking news. I sat straight up, disoriented.

We'd only talked for a few moments when he said, "Hey, I don't know if you're planning anything, but I think you should give it a few more weeks."

What, now?

What did he mean? Did he somehow know about my pact with Lindsay to break up with Jeff if we didn't have a commitment by the end of the year? I hadn't told anyone.

Lance repeated his message. "I don't know what you're planning. I don't know if you're planning anything at all. I just think . . . you should give it some more time."

He didn't reference Jeff or moving back to Oklahoma or anything. Baffled, I told him I heard him, loud and clear, and we said goodbye shortly after that.

I laid in bed wide awake. There was no possible way Lance could have known about my personal pact. The only explanation was that he had some sort of insider knowledge I did not. Maybe Jeff had asked my dad for permission for my hand or something. This didn't seem exactly right, though. Jeff was nearly forty years old, and I was not a child myself. It wasn't his style to need permission for anything, and it wasn't mine to require it. But how else?

After hours of lying there, I still couldn't make sense of it, but in the first moments following Lance's words, I knew I was going to heed his direction. I wanted to heed his direction. It gave me an excuse to buy more time with Jeff. His ring shopping comment had been promising, even if I stayed skeptical.

True to that middle-of-the-night timeline, Jeff proposed to me on one knee just a few weeks later. He told no one he was going to do so. Lance had no way of knowing what he was asking when he called from Iraq.

That the message to sit tight came from my older brother, who is every ounce a Marine officer—tough, factual, and not prone to spiritual messages delivered to little sisters across the world—is what makes this story so magical to me. I might not have listened if I'd heard the message to wait from anyone else. I very well might have chosen differently, deemed Jeff's efforts too late, and rerouted into another life.

I'm glad I didn't do that. I'm glad I heard the words, accepted the message, and walked in faith toward the future that awaited me.

● ● ●

When Jeff and I had only been married for a few months, he was asked to speak to fellow filmmakers as part of a panel at a Texas film festival. I tagged along, a chirpy, blissful newlywed. The person assigned to wrangle Jeff for the day was a British artist named Sarah, with a soft, accented voice and a light laugh. She showed us around town and took us to lunch between Jeff's work obligations.

At the end of the long day, while Jeff stood in a circle, answering questions from aspiring directors, Sarah approached me, asking for a private word. I was concerned a little; her smiling face suddenly seemed serious. I can't remember how she phrased it, but she confessed to being an intuitive. A person who knows things. And she had something to tell me.

Immediately, I was equal parts intrigued and on guard. I had long been fascinated with ESP and people who claimed the ability to know the future, but more than one bad experience over the years had made me wary of those who felt "called" to "give a message." I was curious, but also careful not to trust sensitive words from the mouth of a stranger.

Sarah worked for the film festival itself, and her approach could have been construed as unprofessional, since I was at her mercy as our guide. She acknowledged this quickly, assured me that she had fought with herself all day over this message, was not at all prone to offering words like this unrequested, and had purposefully waited until the end of the event to say something.

I calculated the risk right there in the moment and decided there was no harm in hearing her out. Besides, I was getting better at dismissing what didn't serve me.

Before I could say much else, Sarah started speaking.

"You have two angels, one on each shoulder, a boy and a girl. They are beautiful. They are your children. And they cannot wait to be here."

I grew very still. My face flushed, and the rest of my body went cold. "Only two?" I whispered, as tears sprang to my eyes.

The excited light behind her own eyes turned sympathetic. She put her hand on my arm and nodded. "Only two," she said softly.

I wanted a big family. At least three kids, maybe four. I had it all mapped out. I knew exactly who I wanted to be, and it was a happily frazzled mom of many. I did not see the gift in

Sarah's message, that the possibility of having any children at all was wonderful. All I saw in her words was the lack. I'm ashamed of that now.

"Two of them," she repeated. "A boy and a girl. One on each shoulder. They cannot wait to be here."

I memorized those sentences. They wrote themselves on my soul as I thanked her, smiling weakly. Over the next several years, as one child arrived and then another, and Jeff and I both knew in our hearts that there would be no more, I thought of Sarah often. These two beautiful babies—had they really been waiting upon my shoulders, excited to be earthside? The spirits of both my daughter and my son are both exactly this way. It's who they are.

It's possible that Sarah's message was a hopeful and predictable guess, since the odds of having two children, one boy and one girl, are commonplace enough. But I don't think so. I know how she looked when she said it with such certainty. I know how she didn't waver when I wanted her message to be different. Sarah delivered to me the facts of my future. I see my children now, in my mind's eye, my beautiful babies, Lucy and Finch, and their eagerness to be here with me, through me. I can't explain it. I don't know how it works. But it's true.

●　●　●

We bought a house in a state where we knew no one, on a lake where we'd never been. It fell into our laps, and we never looked back.

Jeff and I both grew up on lakes. My family was on a boat every warm weekend in Oklahoma, and Jeff spent his summers piled into a small cabin with cousins up in Wisconsin. We dreamed of recreating these types of memories for our own family and wanted to buy a lake house, somewhere closer to our parents, someplace where the property was significantly cheaper than in California. I loved Los Angeles but craved time outside of its confines. We wanted somewhere to feel grounded, a place to rest outside the city.

Jeff's cousin Mike, who had shared those Wisconsin lake memories, wanted in on this vision. He was in Georgia, and we had family in Virginia and Oklahoma. Where could we look for a small escape?

Mike was at the gym one fall day, chatting with the guy next to him on the treadmill. The talk turned to lakes and lake houses and the acquaintance huffing and puffing beside him turned off the machine and said, "My high school buddy builds houses. He's working on two next door to each other up in South Carolina." Mike pulled out his phone.

That was on a Tuesday. By Friday evening, Jeff and I were driving through the backwoods of South Carolina, in the pitch dark, looking for a cabin that belonged to that high school buddy mentioned on the treadmill. I was sure we were about to be murdered. Jeff was convinced they just wanted to sell us a house.

Cousin Mike met us on the lake, and there stood two brand-new houses, on their own little cove, freshly built and complementary in style and size. A little family compound dropped down out of the sky. We did our due diligence with a realtor in town, but there was no denying that the houses were a steal compared to what we were used to in LA. Mike's wife, Casey, and I were both skeptical, but the men were all in. We all agreed that waterfront property generally holds its value; we could always sell if it ended up not being worth it. It would be an investment, financially and emotionally.

This house that I thought had come to us so randomly, that I agreed to buy early in my marriage, when I didn't know enough to make such a financial decision, has been about the best thing that has happened to our marriage (outside of our children). I hate to give a house that much power, but it has been so much more than a house. For over a decade, our lake house has been where we've made so many of our most joyful memories, and it has been a refuge in our deepest grief.

We were at the lake when we found out I was pregnant with our daughter after a year of trying for a baby. I peed on the stick and then got in the shower. Minutes later, I ran out in the living room, barely wrapped in a towel and with my hair dripping wet. Jeff was standing at the sink. I can't remember if we screamed or were silent in awe. I just remember how I felt like I would always remember that moment. The towel, the wood floors, the lake glassy behind me.

We were at the lake when we got the news that our dear friend, Ryan, had died in a tragic car accident. It was early morning, and we learned about it on the internet, hours before our friends on the West Coast had woken up. That time I do remember the screaming.

We were at the lake for my thirty-fifth birthday, when Jeff threw a luau beside the water with leis and T-shirts and the fruity drinks I love.

We limped to the lake in the days after Jeff's brother died following a three-year battle with cancer. That was our silent summer. We had no guests, just long sunny days of quiet for weeks on end. There was heartbreak all over that house. Even our young children stayed subdued.

Our lake house has hosted loved ones and new friends. The dearest people in our lives have fled there in their hardest

171

seasons, and friends put a weekend at the lake on their calendars months in advance as part of their family vacations. The grill on the deck has seen thousands of burgers. We've replaced the cornhole beanbags dozens of times.

And of course, we've spent a lot of time on the water. Jeff has a special skill at teaching people young and old how to get up behind the boat on skis or a wakeboard or—his personal favorite—how to wake surf. The breakthrough on someone's face when they get up behind the boat the first time is a true sight to behold. It is an honor to witness these tiny triumphs. Many, many times we've had sheets and towels in the washing machine in the morning while one group bids goodbye just to throw them back on the beds quickly for new guests arriving in the afternoon.

I've spent hours hiding in the bedroom from all the noise and chaos of a full house, and triple that amount of time sitting on the screened-in porch while a friend pours out her heart, tears dropping onto the wood planks. There's something about the proximity to the water that lets people release. It may also be the isolation. Or the alcohol.

I love the house, but of course it's not the structure that makes it so special. The magic there has always been otherworldly, and it started the minute the houses appeared out of nowhere, on a lake we'd never heard of, in a state where we knew no one.

Our lake house was always bigger than just a lake house. We bought it before we could even conceive of what it would hold. We bought pots and pans and decorated the walls with thrift store finds, and we had no idea we were setting up a place that would be a part of so many people's memories. Some places, some houses, are just special. They hold space for something that's needed.

Each year, when we return to the lake house for the summer, I feel sure that this will be the time when the spell will break. It's just a house, after all. I try to temper new guest's expectations for what will happen in the house in the woods, or out on the water. And every year, without fail, the magic shines brightly upon that watery cove. It looks different each time, but there is no denying that it holds something special. I take a deep breath of gratitude each time I walk through the crooked screen door.

● ● ●

My friend Cara and I booked a girls' getaway for the first weekend of 2019. Cara has been my friend since fifth grade and is one of the people who knows me best. She's a surgeon and chief of staff at a teaching hospital in a university town and spends her days saving lives and managing people who are saving lives. My days are almost exactly the opposite of that, and my schedule seems frivolous in comparison to hers. Is it weird after all that to say we are also shockingly alike? I know. It's a mystery to us, too.

Cara and I started taking weekends away together around the time we turned thirty. She goes because she needs a break from the stress of juggling parental responsibilities with the life-and-death decisions of being a surgeon. I go because I just like getaways. For our fortieth birthday year, we decided to splurge on a special spa resort.

I wasn't expecting anything magical to happen. Cara and I had gone somewhere similar a few years before, when I'd been in an uncomfortable place in my life. I had prayed and meditated and sat in the crystal rock cave and just cried out repeatedly for God or the universe or whatever was out there to please give me a sign, send a message, deliver an omen. God/universe/whatever had stayed silent.

This time around, I was hoping only for some quality time with my friend, and maybe a killer facial. Cara wanted to sleep in and eat good food. We were on the same page for the trip, and the page was not magical.

But I was coming off a rough year in my marriage, career, and health. Jeff had been away for months shooting a movie, I was taking much longer than expected to recover from bladder surgery, our home had been robbed, and I was flailing a little bit in my work.

On top of a bumpy home life and health, my fortieth birthday was rapidly approaching. I didn't want to be affected by it, but it was making me nostalgic and a little weepy. The kids were growing up; I was aging; the inevitable questions around a milestone birthday had come out in full force, and I wasn't ready for it. When I turned thirty, I'd been pregnant with my daughter, and it felt like my whole life was in front of me. I hadn't really understood the fuss about growing older. Now, on the cusp of forty, everything seemed to be going by too quickly. I couldn't get a firm grasp on what mattered and what didn't. Just about the time I figured anything out about who I was or what I believed, it changed again.

I had no expectation that the trip would solve anything, but I was hoping for a bit of a reset. I needed a mindset shift. The previous weeks had been rushed and frenzied; the holiday season had, as usual, gotten away from me. I wasn't in the mood to make any big decisions, but my car lease was soon up, and I'd dragged the family to various car dealerships to pick a new vehicle anyway. I like cars, but I was giving way too much energy to this decision. The limbo between choosing another mom car or going for something sportier was about more than just the machine that would take me from point A to point B. I was overthinking it and spinning out a bit. I was analyzing the commute from home to the kids' school, and a dangerous freeway interchange that made me nervous every day. Also, it felt like I was choosing an identity, which I knew was ridiculous, but my choice of car seemed like an outside expression of who I was in that moment. Even acknowledging that this belief was both cliché and about so much more than a car didn't stop me from looping over and over the pros and cons of each make and model: the cost, the fuel efficiency, the luxury. The car I drove was a tangible thing to hold onto as my youth was slipping (had slipped?) away.

The night Cara and I checked into the Arizona resort, I made a final decision on the car I was going to go with and sent an email to the dealership, confirming my choice. Once I was out of my space in LA and on this trip with my friend, the whole thing seemed less weighty anyway. Who cares about a car? I needed to get over myself and get a little perspective.

When we go on these trips, Cara and I book the most outlandish treatments we can find. We like to go to places that are a little woo-woo, that offer healings and readings and cleansings. My first scheduled treatment was called The Path of the Jaguar.

At the end of the treatment, the Native American practitioner indicated our time was up, and said she would step outside and wait for me to put on my robe. But after every massage, every facial, every session that involves someone working with my body, I've learned to ask, "Is there anything else you want to tell me?" I open the door for someone to say something they noticed, usually something they held back. I want to know what they felt in my body and in my spirit. Almost every time, the person has something to say. I've received comments as mundane as "You have a few blackheads; you should look into a back facial," to deeper, more meaningful thoughts about my health or my soul.

In Arizona, in the Path of the Jaguar room, the healer hesitated. Throughout our time together, her countenance had been ethereal, her posture erect and knowing. At my question, her shoulders sank a little. She looked like a normal woman, a friend. She started a sentence, then stopped. Finally she said, "You will be protected in that blue car."

The silence was deafening. She grew flustered and embarrassed. I was in such shock I hadn't responded.

After a few moments, she blurted, "I never would have said that if you hadn't asked. It's so random. It kept coming to me, but I kept pushing it away. I'm sorry it's such a weird thing to say."

I was still speechless for a moment. I tried to squeeze her hand to communicate assurance that her final words were heard and weren't weird to me, but I was still frozen on the bed.

The car I'd purchased in such angst and defiance had been, of course, a blue car.

It couldn't be real, such a specific and needed message. Tears leaked down my cheeks. I stumbled out of the treatment room and to a lobby-like area, where I pulled out my journal and tried to make sense of the highly unusual but not unwelcome thing that had just happened.

Why? Why would God choose to speak to me through a car? Why would the message come from a stranger? It was a magical moment, to be sure, but it was also confusing. Why this time but not when I'd asked for a sign a few years before?

Why is it that people who are dying for answers sometimes receive silence, while I, on a girls' weekend without any real needs, would get a sign that Someone was indeed watching?

I didn't know. I don't know. But just as I couldn't write off the message I received from Sarah about the babies on my shoulders, I don't think the message about the blue car was a coincidence.

If I think of my blue-car message in the context of a world in need, I will fall into despair over the unfairness of receiving a concrete sign while other people, who are just as desperate for a glimpse of a God who pays attention, don't. So, instead, I think it's a better use of my energy to offer back into the world an immense gratitude for getting such a clear message, and to acknowledge that these messages—however trivial or not they are—come when I least expect them, when I feel open but unentitled. It's the only way for me to accept this mystery.

But I do accept it.

Your Turn

The thing about magical moments is that they often defy belief. And depending on your personality type, they might not be the type of thing you feel comfortable talking about. Maybe because you almost can't believe them yourself. It's possible that your storytelling abilities won't do the magic justice. It's possible that someone will offer a "rational" explanation for something you hold sacred.

I understand keeping your magical moments to yourself, but I also know that when I hear other people's unbelievable stories, it helps me believe in the world's mystery in general. And these days, we could all use a little magic.

Magical moments can have a wow factor or simply be quietly profound, notable only to those who were there and can understand that something special transpired. I believe in these unexplainable occurrences, yet I'm still surprised when they happen to me or to my loved ones. Hold tight to your own magical moments, especially if you have reason to believe they won't be well-received. But share them if you're comfortable, because they inspire awe and wonder in others.

Questions to Ask Yourself at the End of Anything

(The end of the year, the end of a trip, the end of a job, any time a little self-reflection might be interesting and helpful. Tweak for each situation.)

1. What was the best part?
2. What worked well? (And what didn't?)
3. What were the best conversations?
4. What was a discovery?
5. Who was the most influential?
6. What was the best entertainment?
7. What are you leaving behind?
8. What behaviors do you want to change?
9. What was the turning point?
10. How can it (or you) be better next time?

Chapter
TEN

What Do You Believe?

For some of you, this is the easiest question to answer. What you believe is your most grounding presence; it's what keeps you sane; it's what keeps you here. For others, it's too daunting to articulate what we believe into coherent sentences.

For me, this is the most important question of all. It can also be the most difficult to express, which is why I wrote this chapter last. Unlike every other question this book raises, what we believe is private. It is personal. Even if we express them publicly, our beliefs are ours to bear.

I believe in many things, every day. I hold all my beliefs all at once. I know you do, too.

I believe in things I came out of the womb knowing, and that I hope I still believe when my last breath leaves this body. I also believe things today that I didn't last year, and that I definitely didn't believe five years ago. Soon, I might believe things I do not currently believe, and that can make all of this a little confusing.

So what, then, is belief? You can't define belief as a knowing when time can prove that things you knew then are not true now.

Is belief hope? I think it's more than that.

Is belief truth? That seems complicated, as not everyone believes the same things, nor do we all hold the same things to be true.

Belief is more than wanting, but it is not absolute.

I used to think that my beliefs had to be unwavering, but now I know that belief works best when it has room to breathe.

It is harder than you might think to nail down what you absolutely, positively believe right this second. But I think you should try it. Get out a piece of paper, sit in stillness for just a few moments, and attempt to write down what you believe.

You might scratch out a few lines once you realize that you believe something for ME that you don't believe for YOU (or the other way around). You may hit a snag when your brain keeps ruminating about all the things you used to believe but no longer do. It might be really hard to keep yourself from making a list of all the things you don't believe.

If you just wait a few minutes and keep scribbling, sitting with it, a few thoughts will rise to the top. You might dismiss them at first because they seem a bit too cheesy, a bit too universal to comprise a belief system. But then you might realize that there is nothing new under the sun. That each generation is learning the same lessons anew. And so the great world spins. Holding tight and letting go.

Believing, believing, believing.

I'll Go First

I believe that asking good questions is the key to connection with others and to our own personal growth. I believe that craving deeper relationships is natural, that our secrets and shame are killing us, and that sharing our stuff will bring us out of the dark and into the light.

I believe that books can shape our worldview. I believe in the infinite power of words on a page, that they can change lives and change the world.

I believe in art as a healing entity, that movies can change our minds, that a painting can unlock purity within us. I believe in the music that speaks for us all.

I believe in love as an act of freedom. Far from constraining us, showing up in love over and over again, in service, in forgiveness, in physical affection, in quality time, in genuine open-heartedness will bring us the peace we're seeking.

I believe in the miracle of my children. Through no doing or undoing of my own, they grew inside my belly and formed lungs and legs, and tiny, tiny, soft fingernails, and this everyday miracle alone makes me believe that anything is possible. I believe in the biology of their birth. Two sets of blue eyes bore two sets of blue eyes, and in their faces, I see their grandparents I never knew, and their grandparents before them.

I believe we all carry the trauma of our ancestors, and I believe we have the strength to overcome it. I believe the spirit is a mighty thing.

I believe in hard work and luck. I've witnessed the fruits of both of these things, the tangible and the intangible engaged in a dance with one another. I believe that either can take you pretty far, but when they are in tandem, there is some real magic.

I believe in the power of a bold lipstick. Don't laugh. It may not be as ethereal as these other beliefs, but an outward expression of our strength—whether that's in lipstick, clothes, hairstyles, or tattoos—has the capability to work backward. It can pull you out of the depths. It can be the "fake it" part of making it until you become—within seconds or years—exactly who you presented yourself to be. I believe this and would look you squarely in the eye and preach it passionately.

I believe in science.

I believe in partnership. I believe in friendship. I believe that we are put on this earth to carry one another. For a lifetime or for a season, I believe our bonds to one another supersede everything else, beyond anything else. I weep with belief and relief over this.

I believe in God. Not the masculine, fatherly God I was introduced to in my youth, but the God that was here before the stories, and will be here after all the words. Not a god that shows favor to one human over another, but a God that is undeniably present in all the things we cannot explain, who weighs the scale of humankind toward goodness. I believe in a God that transcends our understanding.

I believe that we're only here for a short time, even when the days feel like they drag on forever, even when one year ages us like it was ten. I believe that this brevity should make us pay attention and dig deeper. Can we do this while holding all of life lightly at the same time? I believe we can.

I believe in you, reader. I believe in ME. I believe we have the capacity to do beautiful, monumental things in the middle of regular, everyday lives.

I believe all of this.

What, then, do you believe?

Conclusion:
Go First

You made it through a whole book of me sharing my stuff. I've been holding onto some of the stories in these pages for a long time, but I'm releasing them into your care because I believe in the power of sharing to bring us closer to one another. Not just our "stuff"—our stories, our baggage, our triumphs—but also our thoughts and opinions, our belief systems that inform the way we pray and vote and interact with one another.

I think it's important to share ourselves as a way to be known. Because even though we are living in a technologically connected world, depression, anxiety, loneliness, and fear are rampant. We don't trust ourselves and we don't trust each other. And I believe the key to connection is conversation, and good conversation starts with good questions.

It is my hope that the questions posed in this book give you plenty of fodder to take your relationships to the next level. I hope after reading these chapters that your journal is full of messy scribbling and personal revelation. I hope that you texted a passage to a friend and said:

*We have **GOT** to talk about this.*

And then I hope you do talk about it.

Share yourself with yourself by feeling your feelings, writing them down, sitting in silence. Share yourself with others in good conversations, in thoughtful expression, and as a way to be known.

Share your stuff. Go first.

A Postscript

I was in the final drafts of this book when two things happened that shook the world: the tragic death of sports icon Kobe Bryant and the global pandemic of COVID-19, which caused hundreds of thousands of deaths and resulted in stay-at-home orders around the world. My adopted hometown of Los Angeles was especially affected by the helicopter accident that took the life of this local hero, and also as a city that instituted such a strict and early lockdown in the face of the coronavirus.

I cannot put this book into your hands without acknowledging that the horror and sadness of these two things were in my heart as I worked on a book about sharing yourself in a quest for connection. Celebrity deaths often bring a collective grief and a chance to express gratitude for what is good and beautiful, and then also what is hard. As I write this note during week eight of quarantining at home, having physically left my house only a few times in over two months, we're still figuring out how this pandemic will have changed the fabric of our culture.

As surreal as it was to write my first book with these difficult things in the background, my message still holds. Sharing ourselves helps us feel less lonely, especially when it feels like the world is falling apart. When Kobe died, tributes sprouted up all over LA, from murals to makeshift memorials on the street. Downtown, miles of purple and gold flowers and posters and shoes and basketballs were an expression of the depth of sadness of losing someone who meant so much to so many. Online during the coronavirus pandemic, it was a relief to use the internet as a way to share our experiences at home, across the globe, in various states of fear and uncertainty. I think the sharing and the consumption of other people's sharing is the only thing that kept me sane during self-isolation.

You can take the charge to Share Your Stuff to be as deep or as shallow as you want it to be. But do share yourself with the world. We'll all be better for it.

Acknowledgments

An enormous thank you to my friends and family, who graciously allowed my retelling of our lives in these pages. So many of my stories are also yours, and I am grateful for your trust and accommodation over the years as I've shared so much and so often. I've told the truth the best way I can.

Special thanks to Yasmin Dunn, Clint Burns, Megan Bell Bouchareb, Donna Pall, Kerri Campbell, Paul and Katie Soter, Sarah Green, Noah Moskin, Rachel Leonard, Priya Swaminathan, Joy Bennett, Allison Olfelt, Shawn Smucker, Roxy Stone, Tony Jones, Darrell Dow, Megan Cobb, Kelly Gordon, Emily Jones, Ashleigh Baker, Abby Fraser, Kristin Potler, Jen Johnson, Kelly Sauer, Leigh Kramer, Lora Lynn Fanning, Chris Ann Brekhus, "Sam," and the family of Alli Wells for allowing me to write candidly about our relationships.

Teary thanks to my agent, Lisa Jackson, who emailed all those years ago, believing I had a book inside me, and never stopped checking in year after year until I finally felt ready. Lisa, your belief in me all this time still blows my mind. Likewise, to Carolyn McCready at Zondervan: thank you for taking me to lunch back in the blogging years to talk books and for the constant encouragement ever since. I know that none of this was an accident. We all finally got to make something together, and it was the right project and the right time.

To my other editor, Liz Heaney, your expertise made me a better writer in two months flat. Thank you for seeing what I was trying to do when it was muddy and helping me get there. Working with you was an invaluable experience.

For the entire Zondervan team, you made the process of creating my first book as painless as possible. Thank you, Alicia Kasen, for catching the vision, Spencer Fuller, for nailing the cover on the first try, and Harmony Harkema and Paul Fisher, for all your help every step of the way.

For the blog readers and podcast listeners who have followed along in real time as I discovered my voice and message in thousands and thousands of spilled words, you will never know how much it means to me that you were there cheering me on. Thank you.

I have lifelong friends who will be celebrating my book dreams coming true as much as I am, because they've been listening to me babble on about being a writer for thirty years now. Cara Pence, Meg Tietz, Andy Duty, Jaime Hammer, Kimi Dallman, and Lindsay Frawley, y'all make my life better, and I miss you every day.

For the friends who have met me in the last five years, who know and love a slightly different version of Laura than the one you might read about here, I want to thank you for knowing and liking the person I've become. Patty Joy, Julie Stillwell, Tracy Herriott, and Jenna Fischer, I'm just so glad you pick up the phone when I call.

Thanks to the Somewheres, the group of internet friends who pulled me out of years of loneliness and taught me that friendship can be real from behind a screen. And to my work mastermind with Jamie Golden, Bri McKoy, and Kendra Adachi: this book literally wouldn't exist without you.

You shepherded me through, and I'll never be as smart as you, period.

For answering my never-ending publishing questions, I am indebted to these author friends: Shauna Niequist, Sarah Bessey, Nish Weiseth, Amber Haines, Emily P. Freeman, Anne Bogel, and Nora Zelevansky.

Thank you to my wonderful in-laws, Ann and Dave Tremaine, for being so supportive. And to the people who have become our chosen family: Sara Diaz, Rick Kosick, and Shanna Newton. Shanna, you are our emergency contact in every way.

The voices who made me want to be a writer: Stephen King and Judy Blume, and the voices who taught me I could: Oprah Winfrey and Brené Brown. Yes, I am thanking these people in my book. The devotion is real.

To my parents, Lynn and Donna Windel, my sister, Dawn Cash, and my brother, Lance Windel: Thank you. I know you've been mostly baffled by my tendency since birth to talk . . . and talk . . . and talk. But you've given me all the words, and never stopped me from saying them.

Finally, for Jeff, Lucy, and Finch. You are the best part of everything. I love you.